THE
MIND'S
EYE

THE MIND'S EYE

Imagery in Everyday Life

Robert Sommer

DALE SEYMOUR PUBLICATIONS

A portion of Chapter 13 appeared previously in
the *AIA Journal* and is used by permission.

Printed in the United States of America.
Published simultaneously in Canada.

Designed by Leo McRee

Cover design by Paul Gamarello

Illustrations by David Lindroth

Order number DS07501
ISBN 0-86651-259-4
(previously ISBN 0-440-03950-9)

abcdefghi-MA-89321098765

DALE
SEYMOUR
PUBLICATIONS
P.O. BOX 10888
PALO ALTO, CA 94303

Acknowledgments

This book owes much to friends and colleagues, to students, and to people who shared their images with us. I would like to acknowledge my debt to those who read portions of the manuscript or conducted imagery interviews—Harriet Becker, Ray Berrian, Marci Bronstein, Richard Coss, Ilana Davis, Kristina Hooper, Gardner and Lois Murphy, Dilys Sakai, Judy Speed, Dann Trask, and Wendy Yates—and to Humphry Osmond and Barbara Sommer for both ideas and encouragement. Margaret Hill provided invaluable secretarial assistance (again).

Contents

1. Galton's Breakfast Table 1
2. Visuals and Verbals 20
3. Whatever Happened to Imagery? 42
4. The Senseless School 54
5. New Math 73
6. Super Imagers 89
7. Case Study: The Quiet World of R. 107
8. Mnemonics 119
9. Visualization Training........................... 138
10. The Image Therapies............................ 156
11. Mental Maps 168
12. The Colored Compass 183
13. What I Have Learned from Designers 195

Notes 209

Index 225

1

Galton's Breakfast Table

Richards said, "Electrode one, five millivolts, for five
seconds." Gerhard pressed the button. . . . Benson said,
"That's interesting . . . it's like eating a ham sandwich."
(MICHAEL CRICHTON, *The Terminal Man*)

People who think in pictures often doubt that others do not. People
who lack imagery, on the other hand, are skeptical that anyone has
it. A century ago, when Sir Francis Galton asked scientists about
their visual imagery, he found the question had little meaning for
them. Many insisted that seeing "in the mind's eye" was only a
figure of speech and that the very notion of mental pictures was
fanciful. From outside the scientific community, however, he received very different responses. These people readily understood
and stoutly defended their images. They could not comprehend how
anyone could think without the use of pictures. The more Galton
pressed them regarding the accuracy of their inner visions, con-
fessing himself to be a skeptic, the more vehement they were in
their claims. Galton likened himself to a blind man who persisted in
doubting the reality of external vision.[1]

Visualizers and verbalizers inhabit different sensory worlds. A
good imager, whose memory is a vivid multisensory collage, can
raise his blood pressure by imagining that he is running an exciting

race or dilate the pupils of his eyes by imagining himself at the trail's end at dusk.[2] The verbalizer can recall such scenes but only as nonsensory husks. No internal image can make his pulse race or his nostrils flare. Such differences in thinking often go unrecognized. People automatically assume that others think as they do. Disagreements between people are attributed to different assumptions, amounts of information, or economic interests rather than to different modes of thought. The idea that others may think differently from us is at first shocking and then fascinating.

William James, the pioneer of American psychology, remarked that bare concepts do just as well as colored images in running the ordinary affairs of life, but they are much less adequate for recalling a great symphony or the voice of one's mother or for appreciating a great painting, play, or novel.[3] The appreciation of art, music, architecture, and literature depends on the capacity of a work to arouse motoric, tactile, and other bodily sensations. The enjoyment of a short story or novel is increased significantly when one can picture the characters and the landscape. A description of an autumn day is only a collection of words that taps the capacity of the reader to feel the cold chill of the wind, to hear the crackle of dry leaves under foot, to see the brilliant foliage, and to sense winter's approach.

Imagination gives depth to a two-dimensional painting, motion to a static sculpture, and the possibility of traveling into the fourth dimension of time. Through imagery, we can mentally strip away layers of pigment from a painting to reveal the artist's technique and mannerisms. A marble discus thrower would be woefully inadequate if it did not arouse feelings of movement or images of the sculptor hewing the limbs from a large block of stone. The appreciation of architecture comes from sensing the physical forces underlying a building. This goes beyond a visual admiration of form to a kinetic feeling for the stresses and embedded supports constantly at war with wind and gravity.[4]

The appreciation of wine is enhanced through revived impressions of the twisted vines, the hard soil of a great vineyard, the sun radiating down and reflecting from the earth, the heavy bunches of red grapes, the cool stillness of the cellar, and the musky aroma of the wooden casks. To describe what a wine is means attending to its dryness, sweetness, fragrance, acidity, tannin, and other taste qualities. To describe what a wine *is like,* the test of the true connoisseur, revives memories of other wines, foods, flowers, places, and occasions. An evocative memory is the basis of connoisseurship.

Imagery provides continuity to sense experience. "Melody," according to music teacher Rudolph Fellner, "exists only in memory and music is a cumulative art, a chain of sounds through time, each sound taking its meaning from those that have gone before. It is not the art for amnesiacs." [5] The pleasures of musical enjoyment remain indefinitely for the person with good auralization. A person for whom sound leaves no echo must rely upon phonograph records and tape cassettes. Sensory qualities endow memory with richness and vibrancy. At the age of eighty-four, author Henry Miller reminisced about a childhood friend: "His name was Stanley and Stasiu is the affectionate diminutive for Stanley. I can still hear his aunt calling in her sweet staccato voice—'Stasiu, Stasiu, where are you? Come home, it's late.' I will hear that voice, that name, until my dying day." [6]

A writer stores such images for later use. This eliminates the need for returning to the scene physically to recapture the original impressions. Similarly, Miller recalled Laubscher's beer hall in a German-American section of Brooklyn for its "arresting aroma of stale beer, horse piss, horse manure, and other pungent odors." Through his imagery, Miller was able to retain these qualities over eighty-four years. Without sensory memory, he would have lost them within a short time after the experience.

If nearly everyone's earliest memories are pictorial, as psychoanalysts claim, then these memories should be more easily retrieved later on by someone good at visualizing. For those with less sensitive visualizing ability, the earliest memories of childhood are largely inaccessible.

Roy Andries De Groot is one of the few blind food critics. For many years, he has been the wine and food editor for *Esquire* magazine and is the author of several books on the educated palate. De Groot, incidentally, was not blind from birth, but as a result of the

the bombings of London during World War II. His visual memories of what he had seen before then are exceedingly important to him. For a true gourmet, the appearance of the table and the setting are as important as the taste of the food; they are all part of a memorable meal. "I can still see, in my mind," De Groot reminisces, "the first meal I ever had in Paris at that simple and still wonderful restaurant above Androuet's Tea Shop, on the rue Amsterdam, I can see and relive (and retaste) my first Provençale lunch on a terrace overlooking the Mediterranean. And so it goes . . . a lifetime picture book of memorable meals." [7]

People prize their images not so much for the extraordinary events of great joy or great tragedy for which photographs and memorabilia are collected, but for replaying the ordinary, humorous, and poignant acts of daily life. To see again a woman leading an indignant cat by a leash down the street or a pack of pubescents popping wheelies on their stingrays is what imagery is all about. Though we will discuss visual thinking in relation to art, architecture, music, wine-tasting, schooling, and jury trials, these should not obscure the liveliness and vibrancy it brings to our mundane thoughts. It is not merely recalling that I saw junior high school students popping wheelies but replaying their cool braggadocio and gravity-defying leaps that makes it possible for me to share this picture with others and savor it myself many times.

The thinking of very young children is first dominated by images; only gradually are words and abstract concepts acquired. When the child goes to school, where imagery is considered a distraction and a second-rate mode of thinking, the deliberate elimination of visual thinking begins in earnest. The first books we give to children are picture books; then come books with pictures and a few words; and finally books with words and few or no pictures. In theory, this progression could demand greater powers of visualization on the part of the reader. Unfortunately, it doesn't work this way. The textbooks used in school are not written to call forth images. Pictures in the mind, like pictures in the book, are regarded as a distraction or, at best, a luxury to be eliminated as an economy measure.

It has been well documented that the elderly recall memories of

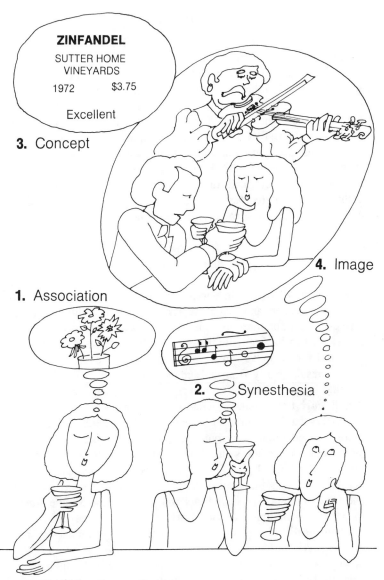

(1) association ("Smells like flowers."); (2) sensory crossover ("I hear a Strauss waltz."); (3) verbal information; and (4) image ("It takes me back to that marvelous evening.").

their remote pasts, including childhood scenes, with great clarity, giving rise to the folk belief that senescence is a second childhood. To the extent that the elderly person uses earlier modes of thinking, sensory memory would be enhanced. The documented loss of sensitivity through the decline of vision, hearing, smell, and taste in old age suggests that inner life might become richer and more vivid in compensation. This would be somewhat akin to the blind person whose sense of hearing becomes more acute. All this is highly speculative, since there has been little formal investigation of sensory memory in old age. Like children's imagery in school, the ability of the elderly person to picture scenes from childhood is considered largely as a negative ability if not a pathological sign.

Mediatrophy

Writing in 1920, Edwin Kirkpatrick declared that the emotional impact of speakers and writers depends upon their ability to arouse images.[8] I am not sure how true this is today, when audiences are accustomed to having their images already supplied. As well, the decline of descriptive prose, including both novels and short stories, results partly from an audience unwilling or incapable of creating images. (I hasten to add that this incapacity can be remedied through training and practice—see Chapter 9.)

Imagery has a historical association with rhetoric. Using techniques gained through memory training, the classical orator converted objects and ideas into images and stored them in familiar places around the home or neighborhood to be retrieved when needed. The rules for images and rules for places enabled Roman and Greek orators, and later friars and priests in the Middle Ages, to perform incredible memory feats. But with the advent of the printing press and a plentiful supply of books, memorization became a trivial art and indirectly the importance of imagery was downgraded as well. Since then, the need for visual thinking has been further reduced by the availability of cameras, photographs, color reproductions, films, and television. The functional necessity for creating mental images and storing them has all but disappeared.

Constant immersion in a video environment reduces the person's need to conjure up personal images. Why go to the trouble of constructing fantasies when a flick of the dial will produce them ready-made? There was a time when a child expected a bedtime story before yielding the house to the adults. Today television is the baby-sitter and soporific. Most adults have lost the capacity to tell a good story. A good storyteller follows internal sights, sounds, and movements. A nonimager knows what is important and can recite general principles but has difficulty describing the particulars, which are the basis of a good story. When Lewis Carroll had finished *The Hunting of the Snark,* his publisher suggested that he include some drawings of the snark. Carroll vetoed the suggestion, since he felt it would rob the readers of the pleasures of imagining their own snarks.[9]

Ready-made images can be discordant with personal images. For instance, a person reading a play and forming mental pictures of what the characters and scenery are like may be disappointed when seeing an actual production of the play or a film treatment of it. Characters in a book are likely to assume definite personalities in the visualizing reader's mind that do not mesh with their counterparts on the screen. To avoid potential conflict, some visualizers will refuse to see the movie of a book they have read. This tendency can help explain the reverse phenomenon of people rushing to buy the book *after* they have seen the film in order to extend the life of the images prepackaged by Hollywood. The book becomes a sensory mnemonic.

Considering that we process a higher proportion of information through our eyes than most any other people at any time in history, one might describe ours as a visual culture. But passive looking is not the same as visual exploration or visual thinking. People are watching more and seeing less. The media, particularly television, do little to encourage visual thinking; in fact, they discourage it. The pulsating pace of programing discourages any kind of thinking, visual or verbal, and the availability of packaged images on every station inhibits the impulse to create personal images. There is no reason for the viewer to experiment with the images—either playfully or professionally; no reason to store them since they will auto-

matically appear the following week and will be replayed during
the summer; no need for visual problem solving or for creating a
personal cinema.

Except for a few children's programs, the potential of a visual
medium for encouraging visual thinking is lost. To reverse this
trend and use a visual medium to evoke images, to suggest movement and flow, requires a different sort of programing. There
must be a relaxed viewer responding to a leisurely play of images
on the screen. The approach in fantasy is that less evokes more.
Used this way, television could become a means of releasing the
viewer's creativity and of encouraging visual experimentation.
Since it reaches people in the quiet of their homes where they can
control their own space-time, television could be an ideal medium
for imagery training.

We are not aware of the difference between what we see and
what we know the world to be. Constancies of shape and color are
good illustrations of this: I see a plate as round even when I view it
from an angle and the visual pattern on the retina is ovoid or linear.
My friend's face has a homogenous pasty color until I inspect it as
if to paint it. Then there is an incredible transformation into
variegated colors, shades, and textures. The painter's eye ignores
the constancies that make the world stable and predictable amidst
perceptual flux. Seeing a plate or a face without the leveling effects
of the constancies is a difficult and arduous activity.

There is a connection between the painter's eye and the relatively
good visual imagery that artists possess. The translation of the
orange chair that I might see into abstract categories makes the
image of the whole redundant and therefore vestigial for the
painter—orange and chair contain all the information that I need
about that object. On the other hand, a furniture maker or interior designer may perceive qualities in it that the painter may have
sloughed off as unnecessary and distracting. The clear vision of the
artist provides a rich store of imagery to be used as needed. Visualization training usually begins with exercises to improve perception, for example, noticing minor changes from one pattern to the
next or asking the person to sketch objects from different angles.

The person who processes what is seen into categories of constant qualities may be able to retrieve the factual information later, but bare of texture and luminescence. This may be sufficient for passing examinations, but it is too limited a vision for the artist.

Leonardo believed that sculpture was not as pure an art as painting, since it required less imagery on the part of the viewer: When the third dimension is there, one does not have to supply it internally. But the viewer of a marble figure will supply movement, touch, sound, and meaning to the experience, a far more creative internal act than is required by the moving picture, the light show, or kinetic art. Abstract painting and kinetic sculpture may demand conceptual activity of a very high order. This makes them very congenial to a society that stresses the superiority of the categorical mind. By making fewer demands upon the viewer's sensory imagination, abstract art—like films and TV—regardless of its contribution in the conceptual realm, contributes to the atrophy of sensory imagination. Films and television are capable of providing a multitude of packaged images for subsequent replay. The problem for most people is that they see too many shows too often that are of poor dramatic quality, and there is little reason to replay them internally when new images are available at the flick of the dial.

Problems of Definition

A mental process, being unobservable, is always difficult to define. Some people conceive of a mental picture as a duplicate of reality, others as an escape from reality, and still others as a distortion of reality. Imagination is viewed as positive when linked to creative problem solving, but it is also identified with idle daydreaming. Its most common meaning is that of a mental duplicate, reflecting the root of the Latin term *imitari,* to imitate: "Ann is the image of her mother," or, used negatively, "I can't imagine what he looks like." As a working definition, I prefer Gardner Murphy's notion of imagery as experience similar to sensory experience, but arising in the absence of the usual external stimulus.[10] The term can also be defined by what it is not. An image, first of all, is not a percept. It is not the same as seeing a tangible object; nor is an image an exact replica. Rather it is a highly selective and personal creation.

There are various kinds of images, including hallucinations, body images, and dream images. Some are completely under voluntary control, while others are spontaneous, autonomous, having an independent existence. Enid Blyton, author of many children's books, described how story plots came to her on a "private cinema screen" during periods of full wakefulness. "I shut my eyes for a few minutes with my portable typewriter on my knee," she told psychologist Peter McKeller. "My characters stand before me in my mind's eye . . . as if I had a private cinema screen there."[11] Blyton was in the fortunate position of both watching a story and writing it simultaneously. McKeller regards such spontaneous images as minor dissociative phenomena, in contrast to the major dissociative phenomena found in multiple personalities and schizophrenia.

Some researchers, when they want to interview people about their imagery, begin by introducing the person to a negative *after-image*. This is the visual image of a complementary color that appears after extended viewing of a colored patch (e.g., a red square that will appear after one has fixated upon a green square and then transferred the gaze to a neutral surface). The experimenter then calls the person's attention to the fact that he or she has actually *seen* the red square rather than recalled it from memory.

Images may also be fanciful and creative. An image is not material, and so it may be much more flexible and encompassing than any reality. I can visualize a thirty-six-foot turnip blocking my driveway or my daughter riding atop a dinosaur with little effort. Most people locate their visual images in the front of the head rather than in the middle or the back of the head.[12] Images can be zoomed in and out without losing the original viewing angle. A visualizer can travel through a microscope and consider a cell from the inside out, pushing his way through the viscous fluid in the diffracted light. The visualizer can also apprehend all sides of a cube at a single instant and consider a building as if the floor were

(1) Pleasant daydream; (2) controlled imagery; (3) uncontrolled bizarre image.

removed and the insides seen looking up from a cold, damp cellar twenty feet inside the earth.

Because we depend so heavily on information reaching us through our eyes, we mistakenly tend to identify imagery exclusively with vision. This confusion occurred throughout a discussion I had with a composer about his ability to mentally hear music he had heard or played or that he was composing. When I questioned him about his imagery, he kept talking about his dreams and his inability to see visual pictures in music. The composer was an audile individual. Terms such as *visile, audile,* and *motile* refer to the predominant quality of a person's thinking. Upon hearing a lecture, the audile will recall the sounds of the speaker's voice and the visile either the written notes or, in rare cases, a visual script internally written out as the words are spoken. The motile finds lectures frustrating. His style is better suited to remembering football plays, rehearsing the operations for preparing a crêpe, or mentally performing a complicated dance step. The motile person is not happy in a sedentary push-button world.

Visual memory should not be confused with visual perception. A person can be very interested in the arts and still be a very poor visualizer. The frantic seeker after visual sensation may in fact be a poor visual thinker attempting to compensate for an inner emptiness. This may also be true of the sensation-seeking teenager who plays his stereo at ear-splitting intensity. On the other hand, he may be playing his music at this volume to shut out disturbing thoughts. The good imager has no need for a constant barrage of external stimulation, since he can create enough for his needs within his own mind-space. New experiences will, however, enrich the picture and tape file of the good imager.

There is no accepted scientific meaning for terms such as *vibrant, vivid,* and *sensual.* A person whose dreams are usually nonpictorial may be tremendously excited by images that would seem pale and fuzzy to a person whose dreams are always in bright color. An accepted vocabulary of mental life would reduce confusion and make discussion of imagery much easier. Use of the term *sensation* when one is referring to the raw material of experience is relatively unfamiliar. Transformed to its more common relative *sensational,*

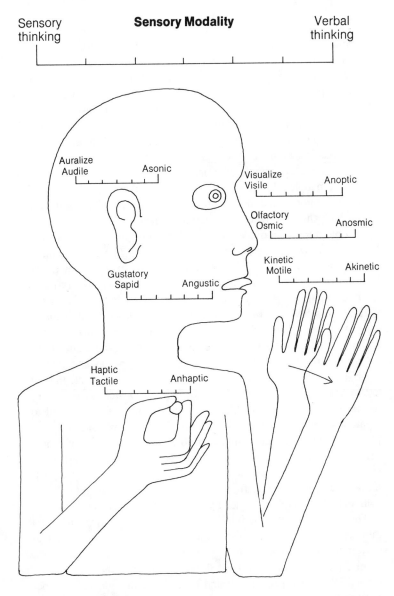

People vary in the degree to which they use sensory qualities in their thinking.

the word has an entirely different meaning. Fortunately, the confused state of technical language does not prevent discussion of the topic with ordinary folk who know exactly what is meant by *mind's eye* and *phonographic memory*. The woman who can hear (and repeat) the words of every popular song written in the last ten years has little difficulty comprehending the concept of auditory imagery. The cook who can mentally taste a recipe as spices are added one by one has no problem discussing gustatory (taste) imagery. As Galton pointed out, people who use these faculties know what they are, while people who do not use them are in the position of a deaf man discussing sound or an anosmic man discussing odor, for whom both the experience and the vocabulary are impoverished.

Autobiographies provide useful insights into the human psyche. People have written at length about what it is like to be schizophrenic, to grow old, to become an advertising executive or a factory worker, to be too tall or too short, very wealthy or very poor. Such accounts are good sources of personal data, but except for the writings of a few memory experts, people do not generally mention imagery. One's mode of thinking is so much a part of one's being, so habitual, that it escapes notice. It is only when the reader finds strong descriptions of the feel of materials, a special attention to odors and tastes and to the rhythm and flow of movement, that an awareness of imagery can be presumed in the writer. There is still the possibility, of course, that these are technical devices used to create a sensuality which has not been directly experienced by the author. A nonimagining writer can utilize words capable of arousing strong images (*musky, resplendent, glowing, strong, acrid*) and sprinkle them throughout a story. While critics frequently discuss the imagery of famous authors, they are in many cases referring to symbols and metaphors rather than sensory qualities.

The lack of attention writers give to their own thinking processes diminishes the value of first-person accounts on the topic of imagery. If we want to know *how* people think, we will have to ask them directly, at least until we develop machines that can do this for us. With a diligent search and some luck, though, one can occasionally find a relevant passage in a writer's notes, such as this one by Isaac Asimov:

I have a clear map of the United States imprinted in my mind and I can look at it and copy off the names of all the states as fast as I can write. When I was young, I used to win nickels by betting I could write down the names of all the states in less than five minutes.[13]

Artist Louise Nevelson recalls from her childhood:

I could go into a room and remember everything I saw. I'd take one glance and know everything in that room. That's a visual mind. . . . I claim that the visual and the projection of the eye is the highest order that we humans are heir to. It's the quickest way of communicating and I think the most joyous.[14]

For the last few years, I have asked my students to interview people about their imagery. We have found that it requires patience and tact to ask people how they think. With larger groups, we often use an adaptation of Galton's questionnaire to introduce the topic. According to Judy Speed, who has undertaken many imagery interviews, the most discriminating question involves the ability to hold the image of a family member in one position long enough to sketch it, assuming that one also had drawing ability. This single test seems to differentiate between those with fleeting, uncontrollable imagery and those who can hold a picture long enough to use it productively. Similarly, Ray Berrian has found it useful to ask adults to visualize the dashboards of their cars. Are they able to place the various gauges in their proper locations? Can they picture the writing on the dials?

Table 1. Galton Questionnaire
(For assessing visual imagery)

The object of these questions is to learn the degree to which people differ in the ability to see images "in their mind's eye." Before answering any of these questions, think of your table at dinner yesterday, and consider carefully the picture that rises before your mind's eye.

1. Is the image dim or clear? (very dim) (dim) (clear) (very clear).

2. Is the brightness equal to or brighter than that of the original scene? (yes) (no).

3. Are all parts of the scene sharply defined at the same time, or are some parts clearer than others? (all at same time) (some parts more than others).

4. Is the image colored or shades of black and white? (colored) (black and white).

5. Are the colors of the food, the plate, the cup, and whatever may have been on the table, quite distinct and natural? (yes) (no).

6. Can you get a single visual image of the *entire* dining room? That is, one image of the entire dining room? (yes) (no).

7. Can you get a visual image of a wider range of the dining room than could be seen by a single glance of your eyes? (yes) (no).

8. Can you mentally see more than three faces of a single die at the same instant of time? (yes) (no).

9. Can you mentally see more than one hemisphere of a globe at the same instant of time? (yes) (no).

10. Can you project an image of your plate from dinner on a piece of paper? (yes) (no).

11. Can you retain a mental picture of your plate from dinner *steadily* before your eyes? (yes) (no).

11a. If yes to 11, does it grow brighter or dimmer? (brighter) (dimmer).

12. Can you get a visual image of the sun high in the sky? (yes) (no).

13. Can you get a distinct visual image of any one member of your family? (yes) (no).

14. Can you at will cause your mental image of this member of the family to sit, stand, or turn slowly around? (yes) (no).

15. Can you deliberately seat the image of this member of your family in a chair and see it with enough dis-

tinctness to enable you to sketch it leisurely (supposing yourself able to draw)? (yes) (no).

16. Do you preserve the images of scenery with much precision in detail? (yes) (no).

17. Can you easily form mental pictures from the descriptions of scenery in stories and novels? (yes) (no).

18. When you dream, do you usually have images? (yes) (no).

19. Are your dreams in color? (always) (frequently) (sometimes) (rarely) (never).

20. Have you ever mistaken a mental image for a reality when in good health and wide awake? (yes) (no).

21. Try to get visual images of each of the following, and rate your image from 4 to 0 according to the following scale:

   4. perfectly clear and as vivid as the actual experience
   3. moderately clear and vivid
   2. not clear or vivid, but recognizable
   1. so vague and dim as to be hardly recognizable
   0. no image at all present.

A glove _____ .

A recent issue of a newspaper _____ .

A fire burning _____ .

A sunset _____ .

When I administered the Galton questionnaire twice to my students, once before discussing imagery and the second time afterward, I was surprised to find their scores significantly lower the second time. Because the students became more sophisticated about the differences between verbal memory and visual memory, they were less likely to confuse their verbal recollections of dinner with mind's-eye pictures of it. The second time around, the students realized that much of what they recalled was based on logical associations and reconstructions devoid of sensory qualities.

A good test for visual imagery is to ask the person to sketch something first when it is physically present and again after it has been removed. This contains a built-in check on drawing ability. A nonimager may do well sketching a model but will fall down, however, when asked to sketch a real object that is not physically present.

The major dimensions of sensory memory are *vividness* and *control*. Vividness includes clarity, intensity, and liveliness; control allows for the possibility of creating novel combinations and of isolating components mentally. A good auralizer is able to hear in her inner ear a particular orchestral piece. If asked to do so, she can move her hands in mock conducting or hum the piece. Full control allows for isolating out particular components, such as attending to the violins or woodwinds while the other instruments recede. A visualizer can recall a scene and notice features she or he may not have consciously observed during the original viewing. Most of Galton's questions deal with vividness. On this dimension, women and children have, on the average, higher scores than men. They report clearer, brighter mental pictures of people, places, and events. On the other hand, it has long been demonstrated that men surpass women on tests of spatial abilities. These two results seem inconsistent on the surface. One of my students, Dann Trask, is trying to unravel this mystery. The answer thus far seems to be that the Galton scale and the spatial tests measure different aspects of imagery: The Galton questions tap the vividness dimension; spatial tests that ask the person to rotate geometric figures emphasize control. Clarity by itself does not seem sufficient to transform or rotate figures in space. Trask's results suggest that the control dimension is related to success in geometry, while the vividness dimension is not. This would explain the seeming paradox of women having higher average scores on tests of image brightness and clarity but generally doing less well than men in geometry and spatial problems. This clarifies something that has puzzled me for years—why the Galton questions correlate so poorly with scores on spatial tests. It is difficult to find situations in which people with high scores on Galton's questionnaire do better than people with low scores. I had credited this to the ability of weak imagers to compensate through redoubled efforts in abstract thinking. It now seems that the Galton scale is a poor measure of the active and creative uses of imagery.

We also modified the Galton questions to examine sound and taste imagery. We have found that the sensory-minded enjoy the questions while the verbal-minded do not. Someone with weak taste imagery finds it frustrating to recall the taste qualities of a specific vegetable, and a weak auralizer is uncomfortable when asked to recall a friend's voice. It almost seems like admitting to a physical or mental infirmity. Their discomfort is compounded by the belief that imagery is not important. It is like being asked to whistle "The Star-Spangled Banner," or run twenty laps, or perform thirty push-ups, or recite the names of all fifty state capitals, or some other task they consider idiotic, trivial, or childish. Those who have been led to believe that abstract memory is superior to sensory memory resent being asked to use an inferior mode of thinking. It is surprising when very intelligent people, who usually enjoy surveys and questionnaires, exhibit impatience and frustration when asked about their imagery. A good imager, on the other hand, is insulted when the questions are too easy. In general, it would be foolish to ask an architect if he could visualize the front of his house, a composer if she could hear the voice of a parent, or a gastronome if he could mentally taste a slice of lemon. It would be comparable to asking a mathematician to add $8 + 4$ or multiply 2×3.

Because we ordinarily pay so little attention to our manner of thinking, there is considerable inaccuracy about its present state as well as its potential. People tend initially to overestimate the clarity and accuracy of their images. This can be readily demonstrated by asking a person to draw from memory a dime or a dollar bill he claims to be able to picture in his mind's eye. The failure to include significant details is not a lack of drawing ability but of visualization. Ironically, people are also mistaken about their own potential for improving imagery through training. Existing imagery skill tends to be worse than one supposes, while latent abilities are better.

2

Visuals and Verbals

When I read a scenario, my first experience is a visual one. I see scenes and situations unfold first on the level of images, and then on the level of emotion. I next try to draw up a draft. The more structures you have to build on, the better you can construct a character that really works.

(ISABELLE ADJANI, ACTRESS)

Most people have fair to moderate imagery. They can use it when it is needed, but it isn't a central feature of personality or cognitive style. There are also people whose powers of imagery are well developed, who approach problems spatially rather than in linear, step-by-step fashion, whose images are rich in detail, texture, movement, sounds, smells, and other sensory qualities. Generally their dominant sensory modality is visual, giving rise to the term *visualizer*. Other people have weak or pale imagery which they rarely use. They seldom dream in pictures and hardly ever in color. Their intellectual style emphasizes words, concepts, generalities, abstract qualities. Such individuals are described as *verbalizers* or *vocalizers,* in that their thinking is a matter of talking to one's self rather than creating or combining pictures. The visual-verbal dimension is related less to intelligence or mental health than to interests, occupation, and cognitive style. Visual thinkers are more concentrated in fields such as architecture, art, and engineering, where spatial thinking is required. Verbal types prefer fields such as philosophy, theoretical physics, or criticism, which emphasize analysis, reflection, and abstraction.

The military strategist who can speak of *only* sixty thousand people killed in a small atomic explosion is either a nonimager or someone with such tight control over his thoughts that he can keep horrible images out of his consciousness. An active imager cannot understand how anyone can watch the evening news while eating dinner. My friend Humphry Osmond has called my attention to the imagery exercises used by Ignatius Loyola to select and train soldiers of the faith who could utterly control their emotions. Potential recruits were placed in a totally dark room and asked to describe various images such as Jesus on the Cross or the Virgin Mary. In addition to sacred subjects, Loyola also used profane ones—a naked, voluptuous woman or a gluttonous feast. He would then ask the pupils to describe the scene down to its most minute details. The candidate's senses of smell, touch, and taste would each be explored. Then the candidate was trained until he could reproduce the images on command. Once this was done, Loyola warned his pupil that if he called this image up any time in the next twenty-four hours, he must report it, because it meant that he had sinned. If the trainee reported the image, he was immediately castigated and flogged, and the spiritual exercises were started anew. The goal was to produce a man who could switch his emotions and images on and off at will, men who were "nothing but mind and will—geniuses of thought and Napoleons of will through systematic schooling of their brain and the marvelous techniques of switching." [1]

Euphemism is employed to rob words of their images. *Poverty* becomes *low income;* the *War Department* is renamed the *Defense Department;* the *privy, backhouse,* or *thunderbox* becomes a *water closet,* then a *w.c.,* then a *bathroom,* and finally a *powder room,* each new word attempting to better disguise the images of what goes on inside. Vernacular speech tends to be rich in imagery. When a word gets accepted into polite speech or becomes sanitized by scientists, it is wrung dry of its emotional, visual, and tactile qualities to make discussion simpler and less stressful. The disadvantage is that terms become detached from their roots and float capriciously in mind-space. No longer do people feel what they talk about. The result is alienation from language. The decline of language is linked to the decline of imagery. How else can one explain such linguistic travesties as *green blackboards, plastic glassware, cold as hell,* and *three-wheeled bicycle?* Such phrases are husks emptied of expressive content. Another consequence of linguistic decline is excessive concern with labeling. It is helpful to have clear terminology, but something is wrong when debates concern only the words themselves rather than the situations and people behind them.

Reading the same article about hunters clubbing young harp seals on Canadian ice floes, the visualizer and the verbalizer have different experiences. The imager conjures up vivid scenes of baby seals being clubbed to death, their skin being ripped off with knives, their mothers watching helplessly, wailing alongside the bloody carcasses. The sensory thinker cannot understand how someone can be aware of this situation and not be revolted. The verbalizer doesn't see it this way. In fact, he doesn't see it at all; he thinks about it. He recognizes that such despoilation is wrong, but his train of association proceeds on to the motives of the hunters, the economic value of the fur trade, the politics of outside intervention, and the two hundred-mile limit. He complains that the visually minded person is distracted by side issues and neglects the larger questions. The verbalizer's freedom from insistent images can be an excuse for doing nothing. On the positive side, it also permits reflection and rational thought that would be overwhelmed by the vivid pictures of the imager.

Vivid images tend to be emotionally arousing. Good imagers who are asked to imagine fearful scenes show greater changes in heart rate and breathing and perspire more than poor imagers asked to imagine the same scenes.[2] However, emotional arousal is not the same as commitment to action. Some imagers are so wrapped up in their inner fantasies that they cannot work with other people or join organizations. The memory expert whose incredible powers of imagery were tested by the Soviet psychologist Luria (see Chapter 6) floated through life like a zombie.[3] By contrast, many abstract thinkers noted for their scientific achievements have been deeply involved in political issues. One man doing volunteer work in a local convalescent home is moved by images of lonely old people in wheelchairs, eager for company, while another visits because of a general sense of civic responsibility, and most who volunteer have a combination of specific images and general concerns.

Misunderstanding can result when people automatically assume that others think as they do. A juror may doubt the truthfulness of a witness with a different style of thinking. The nonimaging witness will base his testimony on reconstruction and association. He recalls a detail here, a detail there, and adds them up into a reasonable account. The visual thinker tends to picture the entire scene and read off the details. The two will react differently under cross-examination. The nonimager can steadfastly maintain the gist of his or her account but is caught up under sharp questioning on minor details (the color of the assailant's jacket, the length of his hair, or the position of bystanders). Research into visual memory suggests that the visualizer will be more accurate in recalling details.[4] The nonimaging witness who cannot recall specific items will lose credibility for a visual-minded juror. Conversely, the juror who is a verbalizer may react with disbelief to a witness with good visual memory. This was the response of many listeners to White House Counsel John Dean's total recall for even minor details of Watergate-related conversations he had taken part in years earlier. Someone for whom memory is a process of association and construction would be convinced that Dean faked his testimony. Witnesses are frequently questioned and occasionally tested as to their perceptual abilities. A witness with poor vision or poor hearing will lose credibility. No comparable questions are asked regarding the efficacy of a witness's visual memory.

There is currently a great deal of discussion about eyewitness reliability. Two distinct issues are involved. One is the reaction of bystanders to unexpected, fleeting events. The second, frequently not recognized as different, is recall afterward. A person may have been a perfectly accurate witness to the original event, but, lacking a good visual memory, will perform poorly on the witness stand.

Weak imagers are accustomed to coding what they see into general categories. How often is it important to remember the color of a person's shirt or the details of a hairstyle a year after an event? Nonetheless, in numerous trials, a witness's credibility has been impugned because of inconsistencies over such details ("When you gave your original account, Mr. Jones, you said that your assailant was wearing a brown jacket. Today you are telling us he wore a black jacket. Were there two assailants, Mr. Jones, one wearing a brown jacket and one wearing a black jacket, or just one?"). Weak imagers are notoriously poor at describing faces. Lacking a mental picture, about all that is remembered is gender, approximate height, ethnicity, hair color, and any unusual features. If there is nothing particularly striking about a person's face that calls for a special label, it is filed under the category "face" and that is all. The weak imager can *recognize* the person upon meeting him again, and may even recall his name and occupation, but would still be unable, after the second or tenth meeting, to give a detailed description of his physical characteristics. Particularities are lost when an event is filed under a general category. If a witness is a poor visualizer, it is very important that he or she write down everything immediately after the event and have these written notes available during cross-examination. The credibility of a witness should not be diminished by the need to check notes written immediately after an incident.

At a legislative hearing on the practice of confining several prisoners in a single jail cell, I observed the different responses of committee members to the testimony. A few senators reacted to witnesses in purely conceptual terms—*click* the witness is a jail reformer, *click* she is in favor of single cells, and *click* she is going to ask for more money. They considered crowding strictly an architectural issue, and the solution was minimum space standards. The sensory accompaniments of gang cells never reached their consciousness. There was a different response from those senators who were able to visualize the scene of twelve strangers confined in a room—no matter how large—who slept, dressed, urinated, and defecated in the presences of others and were always in a state of uncertainty about the intentions of the other occupants. Those senators who could smell the vomit of the drunks, hear the ravings of the addicts in withdrawal, hear the constant clanging of cell doors opening and shutting, who could sense the raw tension in the room, were deeply moved by the experience. To the nonimaging legislator, crowding was mathematical; to the senator who was a visualizer, it was sensory overload.

Table 2. Exercise for Testing
Motor Imagery*

Imagine the sound of the words *bubble* and *tottle,* or any other word that includes *l, b,* or *d.* Observe the clarity of the internal sound and whether or not you kept your mouth open or closed in forming the words.

Now keep your mouth open as you imagine saying *bubble* and *tottle.* For most people, particularly those with good motor and aural imagery, this is difficult. The internal sound of the words come out "thick" and misshapen. Holding the tongue between the teeth while reading is another way of observing one's reliance on motor and sonic imagery.

Mental Rehearsal

Acting out another person's response to events involves sensory imagination. A psychologist asked people to mentally enact specific scenes, such as: "You are an old lady who has just received a telegram saying that your only son has been killed," or "You are a French chef instructing a group of Americans on the proper way to boil artichokes." Their performances were videotaped and rated by judges. There was an impressive relationship between the judges' ratings of the performance and the person's score on a visualization test.[5] Athletes often visualize scenes during practice. Basketball players reported that vividness and control of imagery played an important role during training. Players imagined themselves proceeding down the court and mentally evoked tactics for dealing with the opponents' moves.[6] The important factor was imagery that was both strong *and* controllable. Bruce Jenner, winner of the decathlon in the 1976 Olympics, kept a hurdle in his living room

* Adapted from William James, *Psychology.* Cleveland: World Publishing Co., 1948, p. 307.

"Play Better Golf," by Jack Nicklaus. © King Features Syndicate Inc., 1976.

during the four years he was training. When he was asked why, he said that if he lay on the couch and looked at the hurdle, he could mentally jump over it. He did this often and reported that it helped his performance.

Mental rehearsal is the technical name for the specific exercises of imagination intended to improve motor skills.[7] Mental rehearsal has now reached a wide audience through television programs based on the "inner game" approach to tennis, golf, skiing, and other sports. There is a considerable number of experimental studies of mental rehearsal going back at least as far as 1943, when it was shown that people who mentally rehearsed dart throwing and basketball throws improved their scores almost as much as people who actually practiced over a nineteen-day period, and considerably more than people who had neither mental nor physical practice.[8] Mental rehearsal was also beneficial in a ring-toss task[9] and in basketball free throws.[10] In the basketball study, mental rehearsal was found to be more effective for a person with some previous background in free throws than for the novice.[11] Powell matched up two groups of people on the basis of the vividness of their imagery and their initial scores on a dart-throwing task. He then asked one group to mentally imagine themselves throwing darts at the center of the target, imagining the darts landing near the center. The negative practice group was asked to mentally aim their darts at the center of the targets but to imagine the darts, due to poor throwing, landing some distance from the center of the target. The positive imagination group improved their scores by 28 percent, while the negative practice group deteriorated by 3 percent. Other researchers have suggested that combining mental and physical practice is more effective than either used by itself.[12]

Early psychologists classified people as visiles, audiles, or tactiles depending upon the sense modalities they habitually used. Later it was found that good imagers in one modality tended to be good in others. There are still differences between people in different lines of work, but these differences are probably due to both selection and practice. Art students tend to have better-developed visual imagery, and physical-education students have stronger kinetic (movement) imagery.[13] Imagery should be of most value in sports such as pool, golf, or basketball, where one anticipates the path of a thrown or hit ball. But there is more to games than winning. There is the pleasure of play and of recalling it afterward. The backyard scrimmage becomes in fantasy the decisive play in the Big Game, the Saturday-night poker session is transported to Las Vegas, and an hour's clarinet practice becomes the opportunity to play with the big band in the Starlight Room.

Likewise, much of the enjoyment of sex is based on erotic fantasies. A direct sexual encounter may be spiced with vivid images of another person or the same person committing acts which he or she is not likely to do. For some, such as this character in Truman Capote's short story, sexual fantasy becomes more real than human contact:

> The truth is, I am rarely with the person I am with, so to say; and I am sure that many of us, even most of us, share this condition of dependence upon an inner scenery, imagined and remembered erotic fragments, shadows irrelevant to the body above or beneath us—those images of our minds accepted inside sexual seizure but excluded once the beast has been routed.[14]

In most cases, fantasy is used to enhance sexual contact rather than to replace it. No partner is a perfect lover, but through imagi-

THE WIZARD OF ID   by Brant parker and Johnny hart

By permission of Johnny Hart and News America Syndicate

nation one can transform an inadequate partner into Burt Reynolds
or Marilyn Chambers. The partner, through proper movements, ca-
resses, and words, bears some responsibility for maintaining the
image. The dominance of vision does not hold in sexual encounters. The anticipation of sex involves impressions of smell, touch,
hearing, taste, vision, and movement of an intensity rarely experienced in waking life. The close senses dominate—smell, taste,
touch, and movement. People consciously try to turn off the external vision—dimming lights, closing eyes, being too close to focus
one's eyes properly, and fantasizing. Sexual imagery reflects the
multiplicity of senses involved in the actual encounter.

   Auditory imagery, the capacity to hear interior music and voices,
is widespread, and is probably as common as visual imagery. A
good auralizer can replay conversations held years earlier. It seems
strange that folk wisdom should identify "hearing voices" with insanity, so much so that people are reluctant to admit having inner
conversations. The persistence of this belief is due to the lack of
discussion about how people think. If you ask friends whether they
hear voices, they'll think you odd. Once that passes, they will readily admit they do. What people consider odd is not the interior dialogue but a person forgetting the difference between inner and outer
speech. When I start responding vocally to my inner voices, this is
bizarre, unless, of course, I am holding a dictaphone in front of
me.

For the audile, the writing of a letter is half of an interior conversation. The letter's recipient is heard to read the words aloud, as if relaying the message to a third person. The letter is likely to be written in conversational style, as opposed to a letter written by the verbal thinker, who uses more formal English. Written sentences tend to be longer than spoken sentences, contain more qualifications, and are more likely to be grammatically correct. Oral sentences are loose in structure and grammar. It is difficult to tell just where a spoken sentence begins and ends. There are no punctuation marks in conversational speech and no *uhs, ahs,* and inflections in written English. To write anything except dialogue in conversational style is confusing; to speak written English is pedantic and wearying to the listener.

I have difficulty dictating letters or notes when my secretary is on vacation. Although I know the work will be done as soon as she returns, the picture of her empty desk and lonely typewriter discourages me. I have never felt comfortable having my work typed by an anonymous steno pool. Nor do I like giving instructions about car maintenance to a service manager in a sparkling white smock when the work is to be done by someone else. I feel better if I can see the mechanic who will be doing the job so I can picture the person making the needed repairs. There are also large printed signs on the wall prohibiting customers from entering the service area. Not only am I unable to picture the mechanic doing the work, I also have no visual picture of the repair area or the tools used. So much of our alienation from the world of machines and technical processes results from an inability to picture what happens. The absence of images of someone taking apart a car discourages me from doing my own repairs. My only alternative is to buy a service manual and proceed "by the book." Without motor images corresponding to the flow and rhythm of repair work, the easy play of disconnecting and taking apart an engine, a feeling for balance, symmetry, and completion, I will be a very awkward mechanic.

Like most parents, every October brings me customary invitations to attend back-to-school night, which always begins with inane speeches in the assembly hall by the principal and the head of the PTA. Afterward the parents adjourn to the individual classrooms to meet their children's teachers. For me, the chief value of this charade is not anything I hear, but being able to attach visual and auditory images to names and places my daughter mentions. When she tells me about a biology class, I can picture a short, balding man who taught physical education for fifteen years standing at the front of the room, the green lab tables, the specimen jars, and the nature charts on the wall. The value of such tours and visits is enhanced by a good sensory memory, and cannot be measured by the factual content, which tends to be minimal and superficial during these brief ceremonial visits.

Table 3. Comparing Visual & Auditory Distractions

Compare reading in front of a television set (A), with the set turned off; (B), with the picture on and no sound; and (C), with sound but no picture.

If you are a visual person, you will probably find reading close to the television set—a major source of visual information—to be distracting. Having the picture on will worsen the situation. If you are an auralizer, accustomed to repeating internally what you read, the mute picture will be less distracting than the sound without the picture.

To what extent are you bothered when a speaker moves his or her hands randomly, paces the floor, or displays nervous mannerisms? The eye-minded person is more likely to be distracted than the ear-minded by such mannerisms. The person who thinks motorically appreciates relevant gestures, such as banging down the hand for emphasis or raising the arms in supplication, but is intensely annoyed by irrelevant tics, twists, and twitches. Which of the following would you find most distracting in a speaker—a physical infirmity of some kind, a twitch in the right arm, or a lisp or stutter?

To what extent does outside noise or movement bother you when you read or write? Are the people who live with you affected by the same things that bother you? If not, the answer may be that they think in different sense modalities than you.

Those with weak and unstable imagery tend to confuse verbal with visual memory. This is due partly to ambiguous terminology and partly to the nonimager's inability to know what is being asked about.* Someone who doubts the existence of visual images may be excused for assuming that the questions refer to memory. This sort of misunderstanding has plagued imagery research from its beginnings. It is probably safe to assume that someone who denies having mental pictures really lacks them, at least during waking hours. One cannot be as confident when a person claims to think in pictures. Upon further questioning, many of these people are found to have weak and unstable imagery. A thirty-three-year-old man stated that he could sometimes picture a page of a book and see the location of the relevant section, but the actual words would be blurry or the spot would be blank. His images of the past were vague and lacking in details. When he had to memorize something, he depended upon verbal associations. Another man reported having images, but admitted that whenever he had to recall anything, he depended upon verbal associations. He built his memories piece by piece, using rational thought rather than seeing things in their entirety and labeling the parts. When he tried to conjure up a family member, he could recognize the person's identity on an emotional level, but it was as though he were seeing the person through a "foamy glass" through which the general features were recognizable but the details difficult to pick out. When he was asked to close his eyes and count the number of windows in his apartment, he replied that he would have to rely on rational thought to reconstruct the sense since he could not develop a mental image and count the windows visually. Both these men were intelligent and successful in their careers and compensated for their lack of visual ability by superior abstract thinking and strong verbal associations. Neither would be able to understand how a police officer in Ver-

* I am uncomfortable with terms such as *visualization* and the *inward eye*, which equate imagery with the visual modality. Ideally I would prefer to talk about *sensory thinking, sensationalism,* and *sensualists,* since imaging includes all the senses, not just vision. Unfortunately, these terms carry along their own confusions. I will therefore retain the more conventional vocabulary, with the understanding that unless a statement is specifically restricted to vision, it includes other sensory modes.

mont could apprehend a California fugitive whose picture he had seen weeks earlier on a station-house poster. The answer, of course, is that the officer is a good visualizer who carries around pictures of wanted criminals in his mind in the same way that the anoptic person has verbal information about important dates and events.

Imagery in the Arts

Art critic Bernard Berenson divides people into three categories—those who visualize badly or not at all, those who visualize fairly well, and those who visualize perfectly.[15] He believes painting and sculpture to be most evocative for those with fair to moderate powers of imagery. Poor imagers will derive from a painting only what is directly in front of their eyes, while vivid imagers will find a picture pale and partial in comparison to their internal cinema, which conveys material in many senses, touch, taste, sound, and smell as well as vision. When it comes to creating works of art, all this changes. Imagery becomes a tremendous asset, and indeed an indispensable tool for representational art. To catch the heavy movement of a stallion or the rub of a rose petal requires sensory memory. Literal drawings by nonimagers tend to be stiff and stilted, even when a live model is used. Although not all good imagers are accomplished artists, most artists are good imagers. The major exceptions would be abstract painters who work according to a complementary of form, composers who rely upon computer-generated sound patterns, and sculptor-engineers who work from mathematical equations. Their products can give pleasure to both artist and viewer, but have a different origin and structure than art that follows an internal vision.

Among serious photographers, one can find important stylistic differences between visualizers and verbalizers. A published exchange of letters between Ansel Adams, who stresses a visualization system, and David Vestal, who is a nonimager, reveals the misunderstandings that can occur when two men in the same profession think differently.[16] Neither man could fully accept that the other thought as he said he did. Adams declared, ''I doubt that you

A visualizer and a verbalizer will recall a "Wanted" poster differently.

are unable to visualize, but you are probably not too conscious about it. I don't see how you can control your exposure and development unless you have some objective in mind.'' Vestal retorted that he concentrated upon seeing the scene as it actually existed rather than visualizing a print in the darkroom or mounted on the studio wall. What Adams did through visualization, Vestal accomplished by mental calculations. Vestal knows that a photograph taken in bright sun with deep shadows using Tri-X film requires a particular f stop and shutter speed. Vestal had these calculations memorized and organized in logical sequences. It was not necessary to measure every single setting, since general rules of light and film characteristics guided his settings. ''I have learned,'' Vestal writes, ''not to try to guess what the print would look like, because I am a rotten guesser, though I am not bad at seeing what is in front of me. . . . So when I shoot, I concentrate on seeing the subject, not an imaginary print.'' His reliance upon direct perception coupled with his technical knowledge led him to conclude that visualization was superfluous for a photographer.

Perception, Vestal maintains, rather than visualization, is the heart of good picture-taking: ''The key to clear printing is to see what's on the paper with the same accuracy.'' [17] He advises the photographer to shoot with his eyes, not with his mind's eye. What is perceived in the rangefinder is what will appear on the negative. To imagine something more or something less will interfere with clear perception.

Adams, a multitalented artist who originally intended to be a professional pianist, had difficulty comprehending a nonimaging style. ''I am basically incapable of verbalization of the content of my photographs, or anyone else's,'' he declared. ''If a photograph does not say it, words or explanations cannot help.'' [18] At one point, he characterized Vestal's thought processes as ''too odd to go into.'' He regarded the distinction between seeing and visualizing as ''merely hairsplitting.'' Adams insisted:

> When I take a picture I also automatically visualize the print first. So do you, even if you don't know it. We both see and visualize at about the same time, both before exposing the

film; and therefore both processes [seeing and visualizing] are the same thing.

Photographer Jerry Uelsmann labels his approach *postvisualization,* to indicate his willingness to create a new picture at any stage in the entire photographic process.[19] Uelsmann's forte is photomontage. He takes an enormous number of pictures and stores the negatives. The initial picture provides few cues to the final product, which will be a composite of several photographs, hence the term *postvisualization.*

The heart of Uelsmann's system is the file of negatives, each one numbered and labeled for quick retrieval. Uelsmann works directly with stacks of proof sheets (positive prints of a role of film) which he piles together, sometimes playfully or haphazardly, to provoke unusual combinations of images. Uelsmann describes the proof sheets as his visual diary, representations of everything he has seen and responded to with his camera over a period of years. He deliberately avoids imagining the final picture, invariably a combination of several photographs, when he captures a single item on film. Doing this, he feels, would block his creativity by inhibiting play and experimentation with multiple possibilities. Uelsmann's darkroom is large and lavish, with carpeted floor and a stereo, a place designed for the relaxed concentration to combine varied and disparate images.[20]

Thus we see three well-known contemporary photographers differing significantly in their use of imagery. Adams previsualizes the final picture even as he frames his shot, Vestal claims not to visualize at all, and Uelsmann postvisualizes from a collection of photographs already taken and available. The methods each photographer has evolved in the field as well as in the darkroom are precisely suited to his use of imagery. One can imagine Adams waiting for just the right moment and being more sparing in taking pictures than Vestal, who is not sure of how the final product will look, but Vestal in turn is almost a miser in consuming film compared to Uelsmann, who shoots anything that might ultimately become part of a montage.

Some people cannot think without motor images. Most of us experience muscular sensations when we imagine running, hitting a golf ball, or riding a bicycle. A person of motile disposition experiences movement most of the time. The thought of a car trip arouses feelings of packing, folding and unfolding the road map, the grade of the road, confinement, stretch breaks at rest stops, and diving into the motel pool in the evening. Photography evokes movements of loading and focusing the camera, of setting the flash equipment, and of holding the print in one's hand afterward. Even the idea of an idea, which is considered to be the epitome of abstraction, snaps back the head of the motile individual—aha, insight, discovery!

A kinetic thinker is likely to use her hands to describe objects or scenes: "The vase was so big (raising hands to object level) and so wide (indicating not only width but curvature) and it had a floral design (outlining with hands and experiencing an imagined texture, and at the same time demonstrating the angle from which the vase was viewed)." However, not every hand-waver or compulsive pacer is a good imager. Some speakers move about and wave their hands to discharge nervous tension. Their motions are a kinesthetic accompaniment to speech, but they do not outline or describe anything. One has a reasonable chance of guessing the object of an imager's description from the outlines of such a person's hand movements. With a nonimaging speaker, one can identify the emotional tone and degree of involvement, but not the object.

The sources of difficulty in collaborative work are obvious when one deals with people from different nations and cultural backgrounds. One quickly grasps that business is done differently in Japan, where people have different attitudes toward deadlines, deliveries, contracts, and human relationships. In South America, there is a more relaxed attitude toward time than in the United States, and South Americans abide by a logic consistent with this attitude. Anthropologist Edward Hall offered a consulting service to government agencies and corporations to counsel employees scheduled for overseas posts. It had been found that many Americans were having difficulties in foreign countries because they assumed that other people thought and acted as they did. Often the result was a mutual frustration, followed by a cessation of all but the most necessary contacts.[21]

How much easier it is to accept the fact that people of other countries think differently than to believe that such differences exist among one's own class and kind! When there is a concentration of good imagers in a profession, such as good auralizers among composers and musicians, this is probably a combination of initial inclination and talent as well as continued experience and training. One must recognize, however, the wide range of differences even among musicians and composers. Statements about groups are not appropriate to individuals, and vice versa. To say that chemists and physicists tend to be weak visualizers does not tell us very much about Linus Pauling or Edward Teller. I interviewed two researchers in the same food-science department. One was a professional flavorist with a fantastic nose for aromas. He could imagine various wine aromas, mentally mix them together, and predict the resulting blend with a high degree of accuracy. His smell imagery was vivid, controllable, and useful in his work. A few doors down the hall was his colleague with very weak olfactory imagery. He was competent at smelling aromas and breaking them down into their basic components (fruity, fragrant, fresh) but poor at reviving sense impressions afterward. In fact, he doubted that smell imagery existed. "You can remember the idea," he insisted, "but not the smell." His statements were reminiscent of those scientists who doubted the existence of visual images.

There will be friction when people who work together think differently without recognizing this. Phillip, an astronomer who is a strong visualizer (he invents things and builds his own machinery), told me of his problems with his supervisor. Phillip likes to solve problems in spatial terms, using charts and diagrams. This is very frustrating to his supervisor, who needs to have the computations check out on paper before he can believe them. Phillip's drawings and diagrams are totally irrelevant to him. To most people but not to his supervisor, Phillip's imagery is infectious. When I talk to him, I find myself tending more and more to pictorialize thoughts. This is necessary in order to understand what he is seeing. People who make no attempt to get into his interior picture file consider him merely odd. A computer operator who is a nonimager had the opposite problem with an associate. Ann is an abstract symbol–

minded person who enjoys working with source language. She describes flow charts and other diagrams as "unnecessary eye-wash." The woman at the next desk, a fine imager, considers Ann to be a mental cripple because of her lack of spatial imagery.

Identifying such differences can shed light on the creative process. If, for example, we find that sculptors have good haptic imagery, which involves a combination of tactile and motor imagination, we can try to learn why people of that disposition would choose to be sculptors and whether training in haptic thinking would be useful to students in the plastic arts, and the extent to which this style of thinking affects the person's work and relations with others. One can, for example, imagine the situation of a good auralizer married to someone who can hear and appreciate music, but cannot recall it afterward. Their discussions about music heard in the present might be mutually rewarding, but when comparisons were made with things heard previously or never played before, the differences between the two people would be apparent. As it is frustrating for an artist to describe a painting to a blind person or for a composer to explain a concerto to a deaf person, it would be difficult for the auralizer to communicate ideas and feelings that had no referents in memory for the nonauralizing partner. Indeed, it is incorrect to think of the person lacking visual imagery as blind or the person lacking sonic imagery as deaf. They are not blind or deaf *in the present*. They can see and hear as well as other people. Their deficits occur in memory. The distinction between *perception* and *memory* is blurred because we don't think about it. Few of my friends or colleagues, except those with whom I have specifically discussed the topic, know if I am a poor visualizer or a mediocre visualizer. Because of my interest in art, many of them assume that I am a good imager. The issue of my thinking style does not arise in our conversation. People tend to be unaware of their own levels of visualization and to know even less about the talents of others. The doubts and hesitations that spring forth when people are asked how often they dream in color or think in sound reveal the remoteness of the issue for most people.

It is risky to judge a mental process such as imaging solely on the basis of outward behavior. One could conceive of a person's interest in art as the expression of a developed visual memory or as a compensation for a lack of it. But making guesses about interests based on behavior is unnecessary when people can describe their mental lives. Psychology has certain disadvantages compared with other fields, especially in the great variability of behavior between individuals, but it has the singular asset of being able to question its subjects directly.

An important lesson in imagery research is that one cannot infer competence in sensory memory from interest in a field. Some of those who have been most interested in visualization have been very poor imagers. This was the case with psychoanalyst Bertram Lewin, who was surprised to find some of his colleagues spontaneously generating their own images in response to patients' dreams and thus was moved to write a book on imagery and psychoanalysis.[22]

I have a friend who is extraordinarily good at jigsaw puzzles. She can do them faster and more efficiently than anyone I have ever seen. She has no trouble doing abstract designs, including the can of look-alike peas, the Jackson Pollack painting, or the silver mirror. She rarely bothers to look at the picture on the box and occasionally solves a puzzle with the pieces upside down. She also designs, sews, and knits clothes for herself, her husband, and her daughter, and managed to sell an original sweater pattern to a national magazine. She also did some extremely inventive geometric designs using contact paper for the walls of her apartment and office. To do all these things—the puzzles as well as the knitting and wall designs—I assumed she must see an overall pattern in her mind's eye. This interpretation turned out to be incorrect. When I questioned her directly about her imagery, she described it as being weak and unstable. She could not, for example, recall the color of the clothing that someone who had just left the room was wearing. She could not visualize the exterior of her house in order to count the steps or any other architectural feature, although she could construct the scene piece by piece and give the correct answer from memory. Her method of working jigsaw puzzles resembled the operation of a computer. She had specific categories for each of the pieces based on the little nubs and insets and degree of roundness, squareness, or triangularity. The printed colors and content were irrelevant. This is why she often assembled jigsaw puzzles with the pieces face down. It was not an imagery strategy at all but one of coding and matching forms in intellectually determined categories. Her knitting and wall designs were done in the same nonvisual way. There was a guiding principle, a logic that she followed, not an image. Her designs were extremely clever and detailed geometrical abstracts. She had studied mathematics in college, and her present work involved a large amount of statistical analysis and interpretation of government regulations. Her prose is lean and spare, directly to the point, and free of embellishment and metaphor. Had I paid more attention to these latter characteristics of her work, I would not have been so badly in error about her method of thinking. I was misled by her competence in visual tasks into believing that she was a visual thinker. This does not always follow.

Visual material is not necessarily remembered or even conceived of in visual form. Many people will encode visual material in verbal form. If we want to know how people think, we must, for better or worse, ask them directly. Scientists may someday come up with a more sophisticated electroencephalograph machine that will reveal something of the content as well as the presence of electrical activity in the brain. But even then, there will be no reason to refrain from asking people how they think. Subjective reporting may not be the only source for determining thinking styles, but it is too useful to be overlooked.

To summarize, the approach of the nonimager favors analysis, dissection, criticism; while the visualizer leans toward synthesis, design, invention, fantasy. An inventor is probably a good visualizer; a critic, a weak imager. There are exceptions and degrees in this. A perfect synchronization between people's abilities and their work in all cases would be undesirable even if it could be achieved. There is value in having different sorts of thinkers in all fields, for example, having some nonvisual types in stage design and some visualizers in law and philosophy. Such apparent misfits can bring fresh perspectives to a problem. They will undoubtedly pay a high price for an idiosyncratic style of thinking and regret not having chosen an easier line of work, but in the long run it may pay off. Henry and William James were brothers, one a novelist who wrote like a psychologist and the other a psychologist who wrote like a novelist; each was successful at introducing a new approach into his work. It is no accident that many creative individuals have been mavericks in the ways they approached problems.

3
Whatever Happened to Imagery?

The soul never thinks without a mental picture.

(ARISTOTLE)

Anyone concerned with imagery must consider its value: What is its function in terms of human survival and happiness? The answer must be given in evolutionary terms, both for the species and for the individual, since many traits which were highly adaptive in the past are no longer useful. Skills of hunting and physical combat probably belong in this category. They are vestigial, although the rudiments remain in some limited areas of human experience. Hunting is not the activity it was a thousand years ago in North America, when wild beasts roamed freely. Today, when it is permitted at all, it is a strict rule-bound activity. One can shoot the buck but not the doe, and it has to be a certain size, and one can only hunt at certain times of the day and year and in certain places. The skills and motives in hunting for sport with a gun are vastly different from hunting for food with spear and arrow.

Before the widespread availability of printed materials, knowledge was transmitted orally. There were few reference books, dictionaries, or maps. Cultural survival required that many people learn what information was available in order for it to be transmitted through space and time. Travelers made long journeys based on the verbal descriptions of places and landmarks. The natives of the South Pacific ranged over thousands of miles of ocean with maps in their minds. Many of the descendants of these great navigators now depend on Western technology and have lost their ability to guide themselves. Visual memory undoubtedly had a much more important role in earlier times than it does today.

One can also examine purpose in terms of ontogeny, or the life span of the individual. It has been well established that imagery tends to be more vivid in childhood than afterward. Gordon Allport in 1924 speculated on the function that imagery served for the very young child:

> It permits the concrete "sensory" aspects of the surrounding world to penetrate thoroughly into his mind. The young child delights in conjuring up his images: a parade of soldiers, a circus, a train journey. . . . Such pseudo-sensory experience enables him to "study out" in his own way and in his own time the various possibilities for response contained within the stimulus situation. His reaction, when the situation is first presented, is often incomplete, the presence of adults, or the lack of time, preventing him from becoming thoroughly acquainted with its properties. A period of reflection is necessary, during which he may experiment in various ways with his image, varying his behavior to conform sometimes to one and sometimes to another aspect of the situation, gradually gaining a comprehension of the full meaning of the whole, and building up the attitude which is to determine his future response to the same or to analogous situations.[1]

Imagery permits the exploration of various possibilities for action without the time constraints and possible dangers of the real event. Daydreaming is serious business for young children. However, when they begin going to school, with its emphasis on formal drill and memorization, the need for fantasy as a means of understanding and solving problems becomes minimal if not negative. Sensory imagination declines during this period—not only from disuse but from deliberate discouragement by adults—save for those few young people seen as artistically talented. There is a tendency both from the standpoint of the development of the species and the growing up of the child to regard imagery as a vestigial process—useful at one time but not as an enduring part of maturation.

The importance of imagery was so well established in ancient times that a bitter controversy raged in the nineteenth century when the notion of imageless thought was first proposed. This possibility was resisted by all those who shared Aristotle's view that pictures were indispensable to thinking.[2] We have come so far down the road to abstraction that psychologists who discuss imagery now are apologetic about mentioning a topic so insubstantial and subjective, and if they have good imagery themselves, they don't use it or talk about it.

Analogies such as the mind's eye are helpful so long as one realizes what an analogy is. We obviously do not have cameras in our eye sockets and therefore do not take mental pictures in a literal sense. An analogy means that A *resembles* B rather than that A *equals* B. In some respects, the eye is like a camera and the ear like a microphone. Asked to find the similarities, most anyone could do it. It is equally easy to list the differences between the eye and the camera and the ear and the microphone. Finding differences does not invalidate similarities, and vice versa. Psychologist Herbert Crovitz, in his book *Galton's Walk,* carries the analogy further when he speaks of the possibility of inventing "metaspectacles" that would sharpen visual imagery just as ordinary spectacles will sharpen blurred vision.[3] In no other area of psychology except extrasensory perception (ESP) has there been so much debate about the reality of a mental ability. People who are willing to acknowledge the existence of the unconscious, hallucinations, and biofeedback are still skeptical about visual imagery. Even today researchers must still begin, "Yes, Virginia, many people do think in pictures." One explanation is that imagery researchers have been talking to one group of people and skeptics to another. John B. Watson, the founder of behaviorism, maintained that he had no mental pictures whatever. E. B. Titchener, the father of introspectionism, was a superb imager who never used notes to give his lectures. Titchener maintained that he kept the lecture script in his mind's eye as he talked. He occasionally faltered at places where his notes had been corrected and had to shift mentally to the next line to find the inserted material. It is perfectly understandable that a superimager such as Titchener would develop a psychological theory (introspectionism) based upon subjective reports and that a nonimager like John B. Watson would develop behavioristic psychology, which excludes subjective experience. Imagery is not a topic for those who believe that truth is attainable only in the laboratory.

Behaviorists such as Pavlov, Watson, and Skinner have distrusted what cannot be observed directly and measured quantitatively. The late Adolf Meyer called this *psychophobia,* or fear of the mental. Edward Thorndike, a pioneer in the area of mental measurement, proposed this canon, which was dutifully memorized by his students:

> Anything that exists, must exist in some quantity.
> If it exists in some quantity, it can be measured.[4]

Behaviorists reversed the lines of this dictum. If something could not be measured quantitively, it did not exist. Thus it was that dreams, emotions, and images were banished from academic psychology. The back door was left slightly ajar so that a concept could return if it were suitably "operationalized." This meant reducing a concept to the means by which it was measured. Intelligence became whatever was measured in IQ tests, attitudes became a person's score on a questionnaire, and so on. Attempts to operationalize imagery, however, never caught on. Tests of visualization did not achieve the popularity of personality tests, IQ tests, or vocational-interest tests. The likely explanation is that test makers have tended to be verbal types rather than visual types, and those who doubt the existence of a mental faculty are not likely to spend great amounts of time attempting to measure it.

Some years ago a study found that psychology professors had weaker imagery than their students, and there is no reason to believe that the situation has improved since then.[5] Psychologists continue to be surprised when their students report relatively clear images. This makes it unlikely that instructors will make productive use of the students' capacity to think visually or express themselves graphically. Ann Roe found that biologists and physicists tended to be visualizers, while anthropologists and psychologists were verbalizers.[6] When one realizes that it is the psychologists who, in the division of labor within academic specialties, are charged with the task of investigating imagery, it is understandable that the topic fell into such low repute.

Another self-defeating aspect of early imagery research using introspection was the high degree of psychological sophistication required. The investigator and the subject had to be able to divide and analyze experiences into prearranged categories. For odors, a smell prism was used in which the reference points included *fragrant, putrid, ethereal, spicy, resinous,* and *burned.* Because the specific meaning of such terms was unclear, at least for scientific purposes, to any but the well-trained observer, these experiments often used only psychologists as laboratory subjects. The combination of poor imagers testing poor imagers was not promising, and imagery research using introspective methods soon died out. During the last fifty years, published studies of imagery using self-report have been infrequent.

Imagery has always been a difficult subject to research. The reliance upon self-report necessarily introduces an element of subjectivity. Paradoxically, imagery has also come under attack from the opposite direction, as being too much of the flesh. Those who assert the primacy of abstract thinking consider private phantasms a subversive influence. Writing in 1592, the English preacher William Perkins rejected classical memory training because of its reliance upon profane imagery. "The animation of the images which is the key of memory," he believed, "was impious because it calls up absurd thoughts, insolent, prodigious and the like which stimulate and arouse depraved carnal affections."[7] Western philosophy has been deeply distrustful of the senses, according to Rudolph Arnheim. The eyes and ears are considered deceitful, and the nature of truth can only be known through reflection. According to Plato, sense impressions are like shadows on the cavern wall, misshapen reflections of a reality which can only be inferred through the intellect. Imagery was considered a pale copy of the outside world, a residue of perception carried into the mind.[8] The term *empirical* was used to refer to the quack or untrained practitioner who relied on direct observation and practical experience rather than on theory and reflection. Today, in the scientific community, empiricism remains highly suspect. When it enters into scientific discourse, it is usually preceded by a pejorative adjective, such as dustbowl empiricism or mere empiricism. As the surrogate of the eyes and ears in the mind, imagery has inherited its share of this distrust of the senses.

Imagery is in the unfortunate position of being too subjective for the behaviorist and too sensual for the idealist. Its constituency is found among those who look upon sensory thought as a vital mediating process between the inner and the outer worlds. The part played by visualization in a person's life, quite apart from the value in art and technical subjects, is well stated by C. T. Myers:

> A person with [good imagery] will characteristically reason in a different manner from people who have little of these abilities. Their interests are likely to differ. They are likely to be more successful in solving certain problems. We believe that these abilities can be developed, but they are partly dependent upon innate characteristics, but that they are often undeveloped because they are not appreciated. . . . Spatial ability is an important and pervasive trait, affecting our perception of our environment and our thinking about it. Visual thinking is more than a special technique useful for creative artists or memory experts; it is a fact of experience for most adults and probably for all children. The atrophy or withering of visualization has effects on many different aspects of society.[9]

The main resistance to imagery today comes from those who regard it as a primitive ability characteristic of childhood but unnecessary in adult life. S. J. Segal points out that Galton may have inadvertently added to the stigma against imagery when he concluded that children, housewives, and "common laborers" had more vivid and frequent imagery than eminent men of science.[10]

Galton associated imagery with lower mental activities except in the case of artists, whom he felt never lost their childlike attitudes toward the external world. Illustrative of the view that imagery is not very important in adult affairs is Alan Richardson's statement:

> It is typically of more practical use for me to recall *that* I went to the post office yesterday and left a book on the counter when buying a half dozen four-cent stamps, than to recall *what* the sensory-affective experience of being in the post office was actually like. To re-see, re-hear, and re-feel the experience is uneconomical.[11]

On most school tasks, as we will see in Chapter 4, anoptic thinkers perform as well as imagers or better. One must find tasks outside the typical school curriculum, with its emphasis on abstract thinking, before visualization becomes an asset.

The tendency to abstraction has overtaken even the concept of imagery. When a public official talks about an image of something, it is highly unlikely that he or she means something pictorial. When the leadership of the Republican party wants to change the party's image, they don't mean getting rid of the elephant. Rather, they want to dissociate the party from discredited policies or individuals. In the theater as well as in politics, image is equated with stage presence, or how well a person comes through to an audience. There is very little sensory content in such notions.

A sign in New York's LaGuardia air terminal illustrates the dominance of the abstract over the perceptual: Please claim your baggage by number *not by appearance* (italics in the original). In this attempt to make the arbitrary four-digit number of the little tag the dominant reality in the baggage room, the boxes and bags become merely the shapes and surfaces on which the tags are displayed. Contrast this sign to the one in the Toronto airport which emphasizes seeing: Bags look alike, be sure you have your own. Here the passenger is encouraged to be perceptually active in finding the correct suitcase. Airport planners are working on systems in which all baggage will be containerized to facilitate loading, and retrieval will be done at computer instructions. Should such systems be developed, it is likely that the only differentiation between containers will be the arbitrary number. Most catalog sales offices require customers to order items by number rather than by name. The description of the item, if it is requested at all, is used only to double-check the accuracy of the number. I may think that I am ordering a red widget, but I suspect that a stock clerk somewhere, upon receiving the order, looks specifically for a #9978 and may not even know what a red widget is or does.

Physiologists have identified three patterns of brain waves as they relate to imagery: the *M* pattern typical of the visual thinker, the *P* pattern of the verbal thinker, and the *R* pattern for those who use either mode.[12] In a study of the EEG characteristics of six hundred normal people, two-thirds were of the *R* pattern (mixed mode), and the remaining third was about equally split between visual thinkers and verbal thinkers.[13] Stimulating the brain tissue through electrodes can produce intense images:

> The electrode causes the patient to have a psychical experience, like the memory of some past event, and he can describe it as he lies upon the operating table. The hallucination thus produced may be auditory or visual, or both, but it is neither a single sound nor a frozen picture. . . . Such hallucinations, or memories, or dreams continue to unfold slowly while the electrode is held in place. They are terminated slowly when the electrode is withdrawn.[14]

There were also thermal, tactile, smell, and taste properties to the patients' experiences. In the context of the experiment, the sense impressions could be described either as images or hallucinations, since they occurred without the presence of an external stimulus.

Scientists under contract to the Pentagon have been studying ways of plugging a computer into a person's brain waves. This would give a gunner, for example, the capability of firing by pure cerebral action, bypassing the need for motor response. It would also relay back the brain waves of a pilot surveying an enemy landscape or a space explorer on a distant planet. Experiments have shown that a person asked to imagine a geometric figure, for example, will produce brain waves similar to those that appear when the person is shown the actual figure.[15] Machines for measuring brain waves have the potential, in theory at least, of measuring the presence, vividness, and even the content of visual or auditory images.

Another mechanical approach to imagery is through the measurement of eye movements. Rapid eye movements (REM) will increase when a person is dreaming, and thus REM sleep is considered to be rich in sensory content.[16] Even minute eye movements can be recorded, using new techniques of electrooculography (EOG). When four electrodes are equally spaced around the eye and coupled with a recorder that reproduces lines on a two-dimensional plate, it is possible to measure the movements of the eye in both a vertical and a horizontal direction. A refined version of the EOG was developed by the Garrett AiResearch Company for the American space program to study visual search behavior. A person connected to the EOG tracing out a figure with his eyes can produce a similar pattern on the recording screen behind him. My colleague Richard Coss, who is a superbly gifted visual thinker, found he could produce drawings by projecting an image on the screen in front of him and following it with his eyes.[17] The figure presents the recorder's drawing of Coss's image of a fastback car. The drawing in this case is crude, since he had no previous experience with the EOG. Moreover, he was not able to see the drawing being made by the recorder and consequently could not correct any errors of line or proportion as the drawing progressed. The EOG has intriguing potential for recording an artist's images of a scene almost as rapidly as they are being created. To use the technique, one must be able to create a visual image, project it on a screen, and hold it there for a reasonable period.

Experiments have shown imagery to be associated with electrical activity in the right side of the cortex. Tasks involving visual thinking, such as planning the route to a destination, will activate the right hemisphere. Tasks involving verbal or arithmetic problems arouse the left hemisphere. The obverse effect also occurs. In experimental monitorings, during the time that the right cortex is ac-

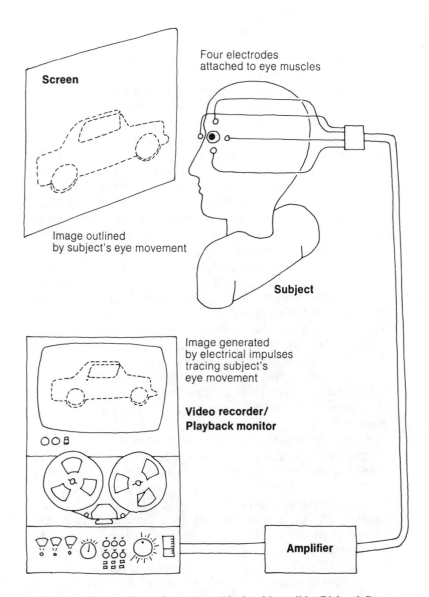

Screen

Four electrodes
attached to eye muscles

Image outlined
by subject's eye movement

Subject

Image generated
by electrical impulses
tracing subject's
eye movement

**Video recorder/
Playback monitor**

Amplifier

When small recording units were attached to his eyelids, Richard Coss produced a drawing of a car by projecting a visual image onto a screen and tracing it with his eyes.

tive, people report more instances of spatial thinking than when the left hemisphere is more active. In one biofeedback experiment, students were hitched up to an EEG machine which was itself attached to a computer that activated certain tones when, in this case, the right hemisphere was more active than the left. Students who were requested to increase the relative number of such tones (without knowing what the tones signified) were found to engage in more visual/spatial thinking than students who were asked to produce tones associated with other brain areas.[18] Psychologists at Cambridge University studied three brain-injured individuals who had lost the capacity to dream or to visualize objects or people with their eyes closed. In each of these cases, it was the right side of the brain that had been damaged.[19] The left side of the brain has more to do with language, abstraction, and analytic thinking, the right side with imagery, perception, and emotion. When people attempt to solve verbal problems, there is a predominance of rightward eye movement, and when spatial problems are being solved (for example, asking someone to try to recall the directions to a particular location), there are more eye movements in a leftward direction.[20] These relationships are quite complex, and not all studies have come out with consistent results. A detailed account of the relationship between brain physiology and visual thinking can be found in a chapter by Vladislav Zikmund in *The Function and Nature of Imagery.*[21]

Robert Holt described cases of people troubled by the appearance of spontaneous involuntary images—"radar operators who have to monitor a scope for long periods; long-distance truck drivers in night runs over turnpikes, jet pilots flying straight and level at high altitudes, operators of snow cats and other vehicles of polar exploration. . . . All of these persons have been troubled by the emergence into consciousness of vivid imagery, largely visual, but often kinesthetic or auditory, which they may take momentarily for reality."[22] This is similar to the experience of people who have been subjected to sensory deprivation. When stimulation from the external environment is insufficient, the imagination becomes more active. Most of the visual hallucinations mentioned in the autobiographies of prisoners and mental patients occurred in barren surroundings such as solitary confinement.[23]

A common interpretation of hallucinations is that they are wild images. Carl Jung believed that schizophrenic thinking was based upon unacceptable impulses that split off from the rest of the patient's mind and occasionally erupted into consciousness in the form of vivid and uncontrollable images.[24] Judge Shreber, a paranoid whose hallucinations were analyzed by Freud, had the annoying trait of playing the piano loudly and singing meaningless songs at the top of his voice. When questioned about this, Shreber claimed that he made a racket to avoid hearing the voices of evil spirits tempting him.[25]

Because serious mental exertion is difficult during long-term confinement, most prisoners are unable to control their imagery and use it productively. An exception was Hitler's architect, Albert Speer, who spent several decades confined in Spandau Prison. When the authorities refused his request for canvas and oil paints, Speer painted his pictures mentally. "Obsessed with the idea of painting," he wrote in his diary, "I have put two imaginary paintings down on paper; strictly speaking, two sketches in the romantic manner, symbolizing my escape world. With the utmost concentration, I conjured up the colors of the painting before my eyes and noted them down on the drawing by the numbers of a paint catalogue. The effort was so intense that I thought I saw where I went wrong, and, operating solely with numbers, repainted certain bits."[26]

Most researchers today believe that imagery is a widespread, if not a universal, human capacity. There may be a few individuals who are absolutely incapable of reviving sensory experience, just as some are blind or deaf, but they are a distinct minority. Under appropriate conditions, even so-called nonimagers can produce visual and auditory images.[27] Most people possess a much wider range of imagery than they use in daily affairs. The issue is not whether all people can think visually, for there is good evidence that they do, but how much attention they pay to their images.

4

The Senseless School

The visually illiterate children of one generation become the arrogantly insensitive adults of the next.
(COLIN WARD AND FRANK CHIPPENDALE)

School, more than any other institution, is responsible for the downgrading of visual thinking. Most educators are not only disinterested in visualization, they are positively hostile to it. They regard it as childish, primitive, and prelogical. Classes in mechanical drawing, shop, and the arts, in which spatial thinking still plays a role, are considered second-rate intellectual activities. The dominant realities in the academic classroom are words and numbers. Pictures, if they are used at all, are there to illustrate concepts. Models, graphs, and charts tend to be stylized representations of reality. Maps are used primarily as adjuncts in the teaching of something else—except when they are being used as coloring exercises.[1] One reason Johnny can't read, engineering professor Robert McKim believes, is that he isn't seeing very well. Class exercises develop rapid naming, to the detriment of observing. Things that cannot be labeled instantly are not "seen" or remembered. Once having named an object, Johnny moves on to something else, the intellectual task of the moment being concluded.[2]

School requires computerlike processing, storage, and recall.

Much of the teacher's job is to insure that facts are stored under the right categories. The visual appearance of an object is equated with a few salient characteristics rather than with a multiplicity of colors, shapes, textures, light, and temperature gradients. The child learns to identify *house* with a triangle perched precariously on a square. The word or the abstract design becomes, in school books and various games and puzzles, the surrogate for the house. The word-dependent child will overlook nuances of shutters, shingles, roof lines, posts, drainage systems, and other parts which make houses work and give each a separate identity. The task of the teacher *should* be to use the particular to illustrate the general without losing the distinctive features of the particular.

The hostility of most educators to visual thinking has its roots in Renaissance humanism. Imagery has been associated with two different movements that are anathema to the rationalist. First, since Greek and Roman times, visual thinking was linked to rhetoric through memory training and drill. The second source of the rationalist's opposition is the long association of imagery with the spiritual and the occult. Imagery represented phantasms beyond conscious control that refused to obey the philosopher's logical rules. The rationalist has always distrusted the irrational. Whenever science uncovers something seemingly irrational, such as a person gaining control over her heart rate or brain rhythms through biofeedback, the irrational becomes the rational and the argument is transferred to other fronts. Although it seems strange that the rationalist should condemn imagery both for its association with medieval scholarship and for its association with the occult, these two movements came together during the Middle Ages, when scholarship dealt with virtues and vices personified in myths and legends.

Learning

Most of the research described thus far has relied on subjective report. If this were the only basis for imagery, its scientific importance would be minimal. Fortunately there are substantial findings

The African storyteller described in Alex Haley's *Roots* encourages images. In contrast, most western teachers discourage children's powers of visualization. Nevertheless, some children, like Susie, continue to form images.

from the laboratory demonstrating how imagery affects learning. Three different lines of investigation bear on this issue: (1) tasks involving the recall of words high and low in evocative power; (2) the use of mnemonic devices based on imagery; and (3) the effects of distractions specific to a single sense modality.

1. High and low imagery words. E. R. Jaensch found that it was easiest for schoolchildren to remember pictorial material that was interesting to them. A picture of a dog or a lion produced a clearer visual image and was retained longer than a picture of a house or a factory.[3] K. H. Slatter found it was easier for a child to obtain a bright image of a simple design than of a more complex design.[4] Such findings led investigators to classify words and designs according to their capacity to arouse clear pictures. Words such as *lightning* and *sunset* produce clear visual associations; *whistle* and *laughter* arouse sprightly auditory associations, and words such as *velvet* and *sandpaper* strong tactile impressions. Learning is faster and more effective when items are high in sensory content.

When people are shown a list of words, those that are high in imagery are recalled more readily than abstract terms such as *word, such,* and *explain.* Experience with a tangible object also improves recall. People who see an actual object are likely to remember it better than people who see only a picture of an object, and they in turn will remember it better than those who only see the name of the object, and the least effective learning will occur if people see only the name of an abstract concept.[5]

Table 4. Abstract and Concrete Words

This test requires a watch with a second hand, a pencil, and several pieces of paper.

In a period of one minute, try to memorize as many words as you can from the first list. Then turn the page over, wait thirty seconds, and write down on a sheet of paper as many words as you can recall from the list. After you have done this, repeat the procedure with the other three lists.

List A	List B	List C	List D
term	sunset	phrase	dog
height	umbrella	more	ring
fill	red	formula	car
send	tiger	deficit	hammer
theory	window	idea	bell
loss	glow	same	waterfall
ask	diamond	code	piano
certain	daisy	quantity	horn
said	chair	instant	motor
element	moon	sort	crow

Interpretation: The words in List B have high visual content. The words in List D have high sonic content. Lists A and C contain words low in sensory arousal. Experiments have shown that sensory words are learned more easily than abstract words. Most people will be able to recall more words from Lists B and D than from Lists A and C.

Learning to pair one item with another is facilitated when the two can be combined into a single meaningful unit. Students shown drawings of two items, either as a connected unit or as unrelated (e.g., in one case, a shoe on a table, and in another case, a shoe alongside a table), could recall twice as many connected units as side-by-side units.[6] Paivio and Okovite compared blind and sighted people using words with strong visual or auditory associations. Based on the finding that imagery assists learning, they predicted that the blind would be helped more by auditory words and the sighted helped more by visual words. Their results came out as predicted. The blind were able to learn the high auditory-content words more easily than the low auditory-content words, even when the latter were high in visual meaning, while the sighted did better with visual terms.[7] Marion Perlmutter and Nancy Myers found that four-year-olds were better able to recognize objects that they had seen before than objects that had merely been mentioned by name.[8] These results indicate the importance of visual memory among preschoolers.

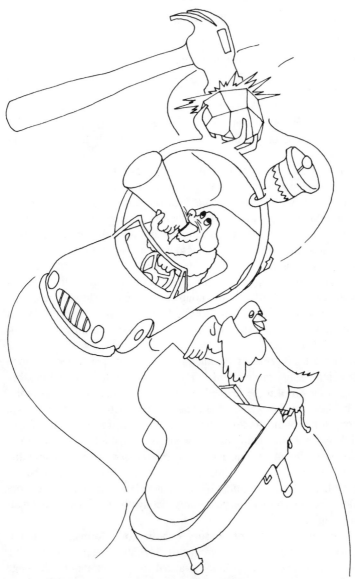

Some visualizers will combine objects to be learned into a composite picture. This picture was conceived by a visualizer asked to memorize *dog, car, crow, ring, piano, hammer, horn.*

2. *Mnemonic devices.* Storytellers, orators, and stage performers who practice feats of memory employ imagery techniques to help their recall. One of the most widely used of these devices is the *mental walk.* The person learns a list of names or concepts by associating them to particular locations along a familiar walk. The system depends upon visualization of objects and places. (A more detailed account of the mental-walk technique will be presented in Chapter 8.)

The effectiveness of this method for improving recall has been demonstrated in controlled experiments. People instructed to associate words with locations on a familiar path could recall anywhere from two to seven times as many words as people using other strategies. The improvement was tangible and dramatic. In the first session, students were asked to associate a list of forty nouns with locations around the college campus. After reading the list once and spending an average of thirteen seconds on each word, the students were asked to recall as many nouns as they could. It was found that an average of 38 out of the 40 words was recalled correctly. When the students were tested a day later, successful recall averaged 34 out of 40 words.[9]

The effectiveness of the mental-walk technique depended upon the picturability of the word.[10] For optimal results, a visual link between the word to be learned and the specific location is desirable. The student who wants to associate *barrel* with the outside of his dormitory should try to visualize a barrel at that location, and to link *leaf* with the lamp post, he would visualize a leaf hanging from the post. The more unusual or striking the association, such as the leaf hanging from the lamp post, the more readily it can be recalled. Images of tangible objects such as leaves or barrels are more easily produced than images of abstract symbols, digits, or geometric patterns.

Concentrating on the sensory qualities of information will improve learning. When two groups of students were presented with a list of sentences, one group was asked to concentrate on the image value of the words and the second on pronunciation. The image group did better on a recall test. In addition, sentences that contained strong images were recalled more accurately than those containing weak images.[11]

3. *Interference.* Further evidence of the role played by imagery in learning comes from studies of distractions specific to a single sense modality. Visual tasks will distract more from visual thinking and auditory tasks from auditory thinking. George Atwood played a tape recording of thirty-five phrases to people which requested them to visualize scenes such as "a nudist devouring a bird" or "a pistol hanging from a chain." After the phrase was heard on the tape recorder, some people were given a visual distraction, others an auditory distraction, and the remainder no distraction at all. Later the person was told the first word of the phrase and asked to recall the last word. That is, when he was told *nudist,* he should respond *bird.* Atwood predicted that if visual images were involved in memory, visual distraction would have more effect than auditory distraction, and the interference would be greatest for words high in visual imagery.

The results were as predicted. Visual distractions interfered more than did auditory distractions, and the interference was greatest for phrases which included bright visual images. With abstract phrases such as "the *theory* of Freud is *nonsense,*" the auditory distraction produced more interference than the visual distraction.[12] In a related study, Bower asked one group of students to use imagery in memorizing a list of words while the other students used their ordinary methods of memorization. Students were given various distracting tasks as they learned the words. This involved a "tracking procedure" in which a student followed a wavy line either with his finger (tactile distraction) or with his eyes (visual distraction). Students relying on visualization were more distracted by the visual tracking than the tactile tracking. Students who used straight memorization were affected equally by the visual and tactile distractions.[13]

Table 5. Learning Homonyms and Homographs

Exercise 1. Read over the following three lines of words. When you have finished, close the book and wait thirty seconds. Then on a sheet of paper write down as many words as you can remember in the correct order.

way	pique	dew
peak	do	weigh
due	whey	peek

Exercise 2. This requires two people. The first person reads aloud the words in List A below, slowly and carefully, being sure to pronounce each word as indicated. Italics show which syllable should be emphasized—*pres*ent rather than pre*sent*. After a one-minute waiting period, the person hearing the list tries to repeat the words in the correct order.

After this, the two people reverse roles and use List B.

List A	List B
bow—rhymes with *no*	wind—rhymes with *mind*
lead—rhymes with *seed*	com*mune*
*in*tern	dove—rhymes with *above*
bass—rhymes with *pass*	lives—rhymes with *gives*
ob*ject*	*ref*use
bass—rhymes with *pace*	wind—rhymes with *sinned*
lead—rhymes with *red*	dove—rhymes with *stove*
in*tern*	lives—rhymes with *strives*
bow—rhymes with *now*	*com*mune
*ob*ject	re*fuse*

Interpretation: The words in the first exercise are *homonyms*. These are words that are spelled differently but sound alike, for example *see* and *sea*. Visual imagery is helpful for learning homonyms either by picturing the words as written or by picturing what they mean, but auditory imagery is of no use. The words in the second exercise are *homographs*. These are words spelled the same but which have different pronunciations and meanings. Homographs can be learned best using auditory imagery. This is a task where the auralizer will do better than the visualizer.

Because more information comes to us through our eyes than through our ears, homonyms are relatively common in the English language and do not cause much confusion. Homographs, however, are much less common. Try to think of some additional homographs. If you are a visually minded person, this will be very difficult. Your mind will be continuously straying back to homonyms instead.

Spatial IQ

Educators are still debating whether intelligence is a unitary ability or whether there are separate intellectual faculties. The question in this form is unanswerable, since intelligence can be defined to include almost anything, and all the definitions reek of cultural bias. IQ tests may be objective, but definitions of intelligence most certainly are not. Test-makers in the United States and western Europe have decreed that musical ability and artistic talent have no place in their conceptions of intelligence. The student who can sculpt, paint, or draw skillfully will receive no credit on an IQ test. Nor will the person who can cook a perfect soufflé or repair a six-cylinder engine. Decisions as to the nature of intelligence have many practical consequences—they will determine which school subjects are considered academic and which are elective; they are used to select people for schools and colleges and to determine eligibility for scholarships; and they are used to stigmatize certain groups of people while favoring others.

Some researchers have identified a spatial factor that is not measured accurately in tests of general intelligence. El Koussy administered a large number of performance tasks to 162 adolescents and found that there was a general IQ factor running through all the tasks, but that in addition, there was another factor he identified as "the ability to obtain and the facility to utilize visual and spatial imagery." This was identified both from the patterning of the results and from the introspective reports of the students as to how

they solved the problems. The tests most revealing of spatial thinking were those that related to the ability to draw things upside
down, spatial analogies, memory for designs, memory for shades
of gray, and loudness and pitch discrimination.[14] El Koussy's subsequent studies in Egypt also came up with separate verbal and visual factors.[15] In a similar study using young girls, Clarke identified both a general verbal intelligence and a visual intelligence,
which she felt were often opposed to one another.[16] After review-
ing work on this issue, a research team concluded that there was a
general intelligence factor covering most kinds of intellectual performance, but that there was also a spatial intelligence, which had
three components: spatial relations and orientation, visualization,
and kinesthetic (movement) imagery.[17] Smith provides an excellent
overview of the controversy surrounding general *versus* specific intellectual factors.[18]

Some of the earliest tests to measure visual thinking involved
wooden boards similar to jigsaw puzzles. When these proved too
cumbersome for mass distribution, they were replaced by paper-
and-pencil tests. A person is asked to pick out a geometric figure
hidden in a larger design or to recognize a three-dimensional figure
rotated in space. Such tests have proven to be highly reliable and
objective and are predictive of success in technical subjects. High-
school students who score well on verbal tests tend to excel in English, history, and social studies, while those who do well on spatial tests do better in shop, mechanical drawing, design, art, and
geometry.[19]

College entrance examinations in the United States and the 11 +
examinations in England discriminate against students high in spatial but weak in verbal skills. Such bias is still occasionally found
even in admissions tests for engineering and architecture schools,
where the curriculum and job performance involve visual thinking.
British psychologist MacFarlane Smith believes that spatial tests
should be included in the entrance examinations for technical subjects, and that verbal tests should be used as *negative* predictors;
that is, for such subjects, students high in verbal skills should be
penalized.[20] Rather than discriminate against nonvisual thinkers,
however, it would seem more logical and fair to seek out spatially

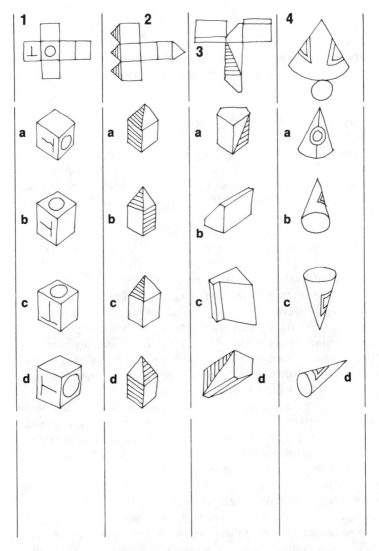

Sample problems from a test of spatial abilities. When each of the numbered patterns is folded together, it will make one (and only one) of the figures on the right. Studies have found that people who can do these problems easily tend to do well in courses in design, mechanical drawing, and art.

bright students. Best of all would be to direct greater attention to improving spatial-visual thinking in all students rather than to developing tests to sort people into invidious categories.

Implications for Schools

The evidence is clear that imagery can play an important role in learning. Evocative items are learned more readily and recalled more easily. This occurs both for the items themselves and for things associated with them. If a concept is inherently low in visual and auditory connotations, learning can be improved by linking it with something high in imagery.

The implications of this for the preparation of audiovisual aids is obvious. The more pictorial the material, the more easily it will be learned and recalled. This effect can be enhanced if the student uses an imagery strategy of learning. University students were able to double and quadruple their recall using the mental-walk technique. However, one must guard against the assumption that good recall means good understanding. The issue is more complex. Most of these experiments employed arbitrary word lists and nonsensical combinations such as nudist–bird and pistol–chain, where the issue of understanding did not arise.

The only evidence that imagery can *interfere* with recall comes from distraction studies like those of George Atwood, who showed that auditory imagery will interfere with the recognition of incoming sounds and visual imagery with the recognition of incoming visual patterns. Like many other laboratory studies, these deal with very unusual situations. In real life, images and percepts tend to be concordant. The major source of interference is likely to be *uncontrolled* imagery. Good imagers sometimes mention that imagery will occasionally distract them from what they are hearing or reading. This is particularly true of poetry, where metaphors arouse discordant visual scenes. An architect with excellent imagery confessed difficulty in listening to speakers who talked too slowly, so that he became restless and drifted into fantasy. Such spontaneous imagery is common in boring situations, where imagination tries to compensate for the lack of external stimulation. Rather than develop a model of teaching-learning based upon boring speakers and tedious tasks, it would seem preferable to improve the quality of education so that students could focus all their mental faculties, pictorial as well as conceptual, on their work.

The finding that distractions are modality specific has implications for the design of classrooms. One justification for the windowless classroom is that it frees students from the temptation to see what is happening outside. Since research indicates that visual distractions will be less significant than verbal distractions when the material is presented orally, one would predict that a noisy ventilator inside the room or traffic noises would interfere more with the teacher's words than people walking by or posters in the room. A common criticism against decorating bare offices or classrooms with murals or mobiles is that they will be distracting to the occupants. However, there is no evidence from the distraction studies to support arguments for a sterile learning or working environment.

It is interesting to consider the classroom as a potential memory theater. Suppose teachers gave formal instruction in the mental-walk technique as an aid to memory. There is indisputable evidence that recall can be improved in this way. This might not be as useful in arithmetic as in history, geography, and biology, where lists of names, species, places, or dates have to be learned. Students could be taught to "store" European cities or famous historical events in various places in the room, such as the doorway, blackboard, teacher's desk, wastebasket, and light tubes, to be retrieved in the proper order when needed. The more differentiated the classroom environment, the more interesting places and objects it contains and the easier it will be to store and retrieve objects. A sterile, barren room with everything in militarylike rows would be a terrible place for a mental walk. It also is a poor environment for educating children. Sensory-deprivation experiments have shown that drab, unpatterned surfaces stimulate fantasy, as the internal processes attempt to compensate for the barrenness of the external. While I would like to see more imagery and fantasy in the classroom, the way to get it is not by creating sterile rooms. A second major finding of this research is that concentration is *impaired* under conditions of minimal stimulation. Any value that a drab room might have in releasing imagination is outweighed by the loss of control over it.

When he taught art students about the works of different painters, styles, and periods, my colleague Richard Coss presented much of his material on slides. To improve the vividness of the students' recollections of what they had seen, Coss developed what he called a "pumping" technique. The procedure is still in an experimental stage, but the results have been encouraging. From Monday to Thursday, the slides were presented to the students in the conventional manner. For the review session on Friday, the room was darkened and the students were asked to relax. To help set the mood, Coss showed a magenta light that gradually faded into total darkness. Then he presented the week's slides at a tempo just below alpha-wave frequency, with thirty flashes of each slide, four seconds per exposure, and total darkness in between. Intense visual images were created using this method. Some students claimed that the images intruded into their dreams at night. Much remains to be learned about the use of this technique—its hazards as well as its benefits. It is intriguing to think of the use of a strobe light in learning visual material and perhaps of the use of some high-contrast auditory technique to help imprint spoken material.

Imagery studies support the increased use of illustrations in textbooks and other printed materials. Ideally, the pictures should be vivid and distinct. A murky, complicated picture of a village in Afghanistan would have less mnemonic utility than a bright, contrasty picture of a street vendor or a young child in native costume. It is possible to use a photograph to convey information or as a mnemonic device, or both. A colorful picture of a native may not add any general information about a tropical island but can still be helpful in recalling other material on the page. Graphic material may also be useful for dividing up a written text and making a section visually distinctive. An interesting question is whether the pictures would need to be related to the text. The reader may recall that on pages 22 and 30 of this book, there were small illustrations presented at the top of the page. Without turning back to those pages, try to recall visually what those figures were. Then try to recall the material on the pages themselves. Does the presence of the illustration help in recalling the location or content of material? The work on imagery suggests that it would be of value, but only if the person were using an imagery strategy of learning.

Some topics are best taught schematically. Photographs and recordings are useful in showing the particularities and uniqueness of something. This sort of presentation is done best when it accompanies visual thinking. A verbal-minded teacher tends to use slides, diagrams, and films only as pretty pictures or boredom-relievers, thus creating the impression that they are unessential. This notion may be accurate when the ideas follow a linear pattern. Yet it neglects the potential of visual aids for conveying spatial relationships and penalizes the student who thinks schematically. Even children with good imagery will have difficulty picturing material that is illogical and confusing. When children especially selected for their good imagery were presented with nonsense words and misspelled words, their visualizations were poor; sometimes they reported seeing only a blur or "streak."[21]

The use of imagery training and mnemonic devices in the classroom has been sadly neglected by researchers. This is due in part to the indefensible separation between the study of learning and the study of teaching. Virtually all research on learning takes place with college students in darkened laboratories, and most research on teaching is carried out in elementary schools. To use a baseball analogy, this is like studying pitching in the laboratory using throwing machines and studying catching out on the playing field.

Table 7. Visual Bridges

Exercise 1. Some people find it helpful to learn things by forming visual images and combining them into a story. If you had to learn the words *jump, tiger, diamond,* and *jacket,* you could imagine someone *jump*ing on a *tiger* wearing a *diamond* ring and then falling off and ripping her blue *jacket.* Try out this method with the following list. Form a mental picture of each word and then link them together in a story.

lamp	jump
milk	yellow
happy	radio
tulip	hit
pillow	sugar

Exercise 2. This method does not work well with abstract terms. Try it with this list.

appear	guess
product	same
theory	idea
more	mental
said	lack

We must still answer the important question of how a person who relies on visual thinking can learn abstract concepts such as negative numbers, infinity, and eternity—all of which lack pictorial qualities. Such ideas are an important part of the school curriculum. Many good imagers attempt to visualize even the most arcane concepts; for example, associating infinity with sands on the beach, eternity with the stars, and negative numbers with an overdrawn bank balance. Up to a point, these associations are helpful. The grains of sand on a beach are uncountable and the stars will outlast the human presence on this planet. However, such linkages are inaccurate, since the grains of sand on the beach, although uncountable, are finite, and every star in the sky will some day burn out, and there are many negative numbers that will never appear on a bank balance. The critical issues are the level of competence needed and whether the image is interpreted as metaphor or fact. For most purposes, the pairing of infinity with the sand on the beach is adequate.

Researcher Allen Paivio believes that we have two learning systems, one mainly visual and the other mainly verbal. The image system is best fitted to tangible situations which are organized spatially and the verbal system is best suited for abstract material that is organized sequentially.[22] Young children rely initially on sensory and motoric images for representing the world, but these become superseded and pushed aside by the child's developing linguistic competence.[23] There is a gradual withering away of an imagination starved by neglect and disuse. Visual impressions are no longer remembered with their full pungency when they are stored as concepts drained of sensory content.

Studies comparing the school performance of good and poor imagers have yielded ambiguous results. For the most part, nonimagers are able to compensate for their deficits by emphasizing nonvisual memory. This is a familiar situation in the psychology laboratory, where people are able to compensate, and often to overcompensate, for small doses of drugs, noise, and moderate cold or heat. It is extraordinarily difficult to find tasks on which motivated, healthy people cannot compensate for gaps in one area by doubling their efforts in another. There is no evidence linking good imagery with intelligence or general school performance. Most authorities believe that if there is such a relationship, it is probably a negative one, with the visualizer being handicapped in comparison to the verbal thinker: School curricula that emphasize classification and categorical thinking are likely to penalize the visualizer and favor the verbalizer. One has to examine specific subjects that involve spatial thinking, such as mechanical drawing, art, music, engineering, and various shop courses before the benefits of pictorial thinking become apparent.

What has motivated recent researchers is the belief that imagery can co-exist with abstract thinking and become a helpful tool in problem solving. There is ample evidence that working with the child's capacity to visualize rather than suppressing it will produce more effective learning. This does not mean that school curricula should be dominated by pictorial modes of instruction. A curriculum intent solely upon developing imagery to the neglect of classification and analysis would be worse than useless. Life today is far too complex to be dominated by unchangeable images. When Galton found that scientists tended to have poor imagery, he did not dismiss visualization as a useless or inferior mental ability. Instead, he maintained that the highest development of human intellect meant the availability of imagery for use in those situations where it was needed. Attempts to downgrade all those subjects involving spatial thinking will prevent the fullest realization of the human potential. It is a mistake to talk about abstract *versus* verbal thinking, just as it is foolish to speak of seeing *versus* touch or *versus* smell. Only in the most unusual situations are mental faculties antagonistic to one another, and such rare instances should not be the models for school curricula. Classrooms encourage a schizoid detachment on the part of students who must suppress all impulses to see, do, move about, or feel anything. Sit-and-listen instruction tends to be "senseless" teaching.

Although I have never seen this actually tested, I suspect that students could do just as well sitting in English, history, and social studies classes with their eyes closed. The small amount of writing on the board—usually words, since few teachers will attempt to actually draw anything more complicated than a circle or square—are also described orally. A deaf child will have more problems in school than will a blind child. In many respects, teachers treat all children as if they were blind. With respect to visual imagery, they push them to be blind.

5

New Math

> In today's books, mathematics is a game with twenty-six letters that mean nothing.
>
> (HANS FREUDENTHAL)

New math is new no longer; its reputation is somewhat tarnished; its supporters are beleaguered and bruised from encounters with irate parents and legislators. Results from its application in elementary and high schools are mixed at best. A recent summary concludes that students using the new math do neither better nor worse than students using traditional methods. Nor are they more positive in their attitudes toward mathematics.[1] School districts across the country, once having eagerly responded to the innovative curriculum, are now either discarding it or drastically overhauling it. The reasons for its failure, or, more generously, its lack of success, are directly related to the topics we have discussed thus far. More specifically, new math failed because of its bias toward abstraction and its devaluation of imagery.

The curriculum was developed not by elementary teachers who wanted to help their students learn arithmetic better but by college educators and professional mathematicians. Financial support came from the National Science Foundation and other government agencies jolted by the apparent "learning gap" signaled by the Soviet

Sputnik program. In the logic of the Cold War, new math was seen as a way of winning the brain race with Communist nations by exposing young children to the ideas of advanced mathematics at an early age. The goal of its developers was to make the beginning study of the subject more abstract by emphasizing key concepts, essential features, and basic structures. Adjectives such as *key, essential,* and *basic* indicate the concern with ideas beyond and more important than what can be apprehended by the senses. It was hoped that removing mathematical concepts from tangible objects would increase their generality. The distinction between *numbers* and *numerals* was emphasized. The child was taught that a numeral was the written symbol, a number the ideal abstraction. "Three" no longer existed in the real world; it was only a numerical symbol. A textbook for teachers of the new math states this succinctly: "To a mathematician a *number* is an idea. . . . One cannot see, write, or draw a *number.*" [2]

No longer was arithmetic to be judged in terms of its correspondence to the physical world. There could be negative numbers and infinite quantities. Arithmeticians of earlier times resisted the notion of negative numbers, since they did not exist in the real world. But on the plane of abstraction, any number is possible so long as it follows certain logical principles. Mathematics made a tremendous leap when it went beyond the senses to detached principles. However, the relevance of this for teaching mathematics in elementary school became the crux of the controversy surrounding what its advocates described as a revolution in school mathematics. [3]

The basis of geometry in the new math is the *point,* an idealized expression without length, width, or depth. A point can neither be felt, seen, nor measured. [4] The basis of both numbers and points under the new system is that they are unimaginable. It is the specific task of the new-math teacher to dissolve any connection between concepts and the material world. This may not be evident to the visitor who sees students in class exercises using beads, buttons, and apples. Appearances, however, are deceiving. Such exercises look perceptual but they are not. Their objective in the new math is to demonstrate to the pupil that three buttons, three beads, and three apples are each representative of the number-set three. Eventually three becomes detached from anything that can be seen, felt, or tasted. For a student whose images have survived the initial onslaught of idealized categories, the "other bases" computations deliver the *coup de grâce*. Computed in the base four, the numeral 12 represents six objects, not twelve. In the base five, it represents seven objects. Pictorial thinking is a hindrance in this system.

Detachment from practical application was not an incidental by-product of the new math but a deliberate goal. Practical issues were considered impediments to a pure abstraction. The term *meaningful math*, which was sometimes applied to the new methods, referred to conceptual logic. A student was supposed to appreciate the consistency and order of a series without reference to the facts of experience. A book by two proponents of the new math justifies the downgrading of practical application in the curriculum:

> More time for studying new topics has been attained by cutting down on the application of mathematics in business, home, and government. Topics such as banking, budgets, stocks and bonds, installment buying, taxation, and insurance are no longer considered a suitable content for mathematics. These social applications have been eliminated for several reasons. They merely require computation, usually with percents and decimals. They are best dealt with in connection with fractions and ratios, without involving the social situation. And the social aspects of these topics can better be treated in social science or business courses—or perhaps by parents. Furthermore, in these changing times, when computing machines are performing many routine mathematical computations, the applications of today may be unimportant in the future.[5]

Memory drill and calculating skills were both important in a classical education. It is not surprising that as one was downgraded, so was the other. The same arguments directed against memory drill were also used to condemn practice in multiplication, addition, subtraction, and division. Advocates of the new rationalism maintained that an understanding of principles was more important to the learner than being able to perform the operations. Several decades ago a store clerk had to be able to add figures in her head or on paper. Today most of these calculations are done by machine. Computational skill, like the ability to remember things, is considered vestigial and second-rate, since it presumably can be done more quickly and accurately by machine. This is both true and not true, however; that is the paradox. The difference is whether one views machines as extensions of people who understand what they are doing, or people as the unknowing extensions of machines. As a college teacher, I find nothing more pathetic than the graduate student who has just gotten an enormous stack of computer printouts and doesn't have the foggiest notion of what they mean. The sheer weight of calculations produced by the computer tends to destroy the connection between the numbers and what they represent. This makes it almost inevitable that the student will lose sight of the original problem, and the means become the ends.

Had the new math developed solely as an approach for college students, its introduction might have aroused little controversy. Unfortunately, the main push came in the elementary schools when, in the view of many developmental psychologists, young children are not ready for abstract ideas. In Jean Piaget's theory of cognitive development, grammar-school children are at the stage of concrete operations: They learn best what appeals to the senses. Only later, when they have developed a sufficient base of tangible experiences, will they be able to handle detached ideas.[6] The young child doesn't see *six;* he or she sees six oranges or six flowers or six people. Children are not simply little adults with the identical mental makeup but knowing less than big people; instead they often use qualitatively different modes of processing information.

Whether new math can be adjusted to fit the different stages of intellectual growth is only part of the issue. The larger question—which is the hidden agenda of the new math—is the long-range impact of devaluing perception. To the extent that it dissolved the connection between numbers and images, new math was single-minded in its approach. It tried to develop understanding *at the expense of the senses.*

A mathematical statement leaves the hearer cold when it evokes no images or associations. It is as if the words were uttered in a foreign language. Indeed, mathematics is often taught as if it were a foreign language, with only the most arbitrary connection between symbols and objects. There is nothing in a number that suggests its meaning to the learner.[7] This was not always the case. Many of the ancient systems for learning numbers, such as the Egyptian, were pictorial. The chief problem today is not that our numerals lack pictorial qualities. It is fairly easy, as many educational films have done, to make cartoons of numerals—tall, straight Mr. One; bent-over, old Ms. Two; the potbelly of Mr. Five; and so on. The problem is not the symbols themselves, but that our teaching of arithmetic detaches numbers from the stuff of life. Without images behind the figures, the person doing the calculations forgets what the terms signify. When an occasional absurd result is produced through arithmetic error, the person presents it as the answer without any hesitation. I have seen otherwise intelligent students turn in bizarre arithmetic solutions which they never would have considered acceptable if they had been using words instead of numbers. It was as if they were stringing together foreign terms according to some set of rules, without any idea what the words meant.

I will acknowledge the need for nonimageable terms in higher mathematics and advanced research. Some of the distances involved in space exploration are so large that they cannot refer to anything in a person's experience. I hope that this is not always the case. Numbers such as *millions,* which make sense to us, would have been incomprehensible to our ancestors. When my grandchildren learn the distances in our solar system and beyond, I hope they can connect them to actual items in their experience. I recall being impressed by a news report that the diameter of a distant star is as large as our entire solar system. I think I can encompass this in a mental map or schema. For anything larger than this, I draw a blank in terms of images and associations. This does not prevent me from combining nonimageable numbers according to various rules. I know that the product of 10^{200} and 10^{400} is 10^{600}. These figures have no images or associations for me. This is not necessarily the case for someone who works with quantities of this magnitude and knows their properties. Familiarity endows numbers with emo-

Egyptian symbol	Meaning	Arabic symbol
|	Vertical Stroke	1
∩	Heel Bone	10
⌒	Coil of Rope	100
𓆼	Lotus Flower	1,000
⌒	Pointing Finger	10,000
⊂	Burbot Fish	100,000
𓀠	Man in Astonishment	1,000,000

3203 = 𓆼𓆼𓆼 ⌒⌒ \|\|\|

Egyptian picture-numbers and their Arabic equivalents.

tional and animistic properties, occasionally with color or tactual synethesias. The number *8* may seem like a good friend, solid and reliable, *143* as if it had a part missing, and *9900* forceful and domineering. Such associations can relate to more complex properties. When mathematician G. H. Hardy visited his Indian protégé, Srinivasa Ramanujan, who was sick in bed, Hardy casually mentioned that the taxicab number had been 1729, adding, "A rather dull number, isn't it?" "Not at all," Ramanujan, who had personal regard for all numbers, replied. "It is the smallest number expressible as the sum of two cubes in two different ways." ($1^3 + 12^3 = 9^3 + 10^3 = 1729$).[8] For those who care about them, number systems are elegant, personable, and personal. Abstract, yes, but much more.

Table 8. Lightning Calculation

One of the most impressive demonstrations of arithmetical prodigies involves squaring numbers such as 9,999. This is incredibly time consuming on paper, and most of us would find it impossible to do in our heads. A simple extension of the binomial theorem makes it easy to do mentally or on paper.

$(a-b)^2 = a^2 + b^2 - 2ab$.
Using this formula means transforming 9,999 into $10,000 - 1$.
Therefore, $(10,000 - 1)^2 = 10,000^2 + 1^2 - 2 (1 \times 10,000)$
Continuing: $100,000,000 + 1 - 20,000 = 99,980,001$.
It is even easier to square $a + b$. This becomes $a^2 + b^2 + 2ab$.

One immediately converts $(53)^2$ into $(50 + 3)^2$ which becomes $2,500 + 9 + 2 (50 \times 3)$. This method can be used as $a - b$, or $a + b$, whichever is easier. That is, 53 can be converted to $50 + 3$ or $60 - 7$.

Using this method, mentally square each of the following numbers: 48, 62, 109, 9,999, 10,006. These numbers can all be done easily in the mind's eye because they break up into combinations that are easily handled. To use this method routinely would require immediate knowledge of all possible products of all one- and two-digit numbers. Squaring 838 using this method requires knowing the square of 8 (that is easy), but also the square of 38 *and* the product of 8 and 38. If one does not have these figures readily available, the method is cumbersome and inefficient.

Vastly different from the approach of the new math is that taken in the art class where the student sketching an apple learns to appreciate subtle variations in shape, hue, and shadow. Artists need images of the particular because their subject is unique. But the work of the artist is more than registering on canvas literally what appears before the eyes; the artist reveals the general in the particular and the particular in the general. The serious artist undertakes considerable research before beginning a major work. A portrait will be enriched when the artist knows something about the life of the subject. The bias against imagery in the schools can be corrected without discarding the faculty for abstract thought. The math teacher's example of three apples as a number-set need not obscure the artist's view of each apple as unique. The human potential includes the facility for both algebra and art.

Jacques Hadamard asked Albert Einstein about his methods of thought. Einstein replied:

> The words or the language do not seem to play any role in my mechanism of thought. The physical entities which seem to serve as elements in thought are certain signs and more or less clear images which can be voluntarily reproduced and combined. . . . It is also clear that the desire to arrive finally at logically connected concepts is the emotional basis of this rather vague play with the above mentioned elements.[9]

Based on his writings, I would guess that mathematician Rózsa Péter is a developed haptic thinker. Haptic imagery involves a combination of tactile and motor imagination. Péter describes the goals of the mathematics teacher as "clarifying the essential points so that they hit the eye, and who himself knows the joy of mathematical creation and writes with such a swing that he carries the reader along with him." [10] Péter teaches counting as rhythmic repetitive play to compare the development of a number system to the poet's use of rhyme and alliteration. Motor imagery includes a feeling for flow and pattern useful in even the higher reaches of abstraction. To empty numbers of their sensory content is to deny children the feeling for the beauty and play of sequence, series, and powers.

Students today are discouraged from solving geometry and other mathematical problems in their heads. Instead they are told to work things out on paper, indicating every step along the way. This is supposed to permit the teacher and pupil to see exactly where an error was made. Solving problems on paper makes mental solutions unnecessary, and frequently the formalized methods of a paper solution will be different from the operations involved in a visual solution. Faced with this conflict between the teacher's requirements for a written solution and the possibility of arriving at a mental solution, the child learns to ignore imagery and concentrate on abstract operations. A good imager I interviewed mentioned the problems he had in courses in which his teachers complained that he didn't do the intermediate steps. His response was that he did the preliminaries in his mind's eye and put only the solution on the paper. He also admitted his difficulties in algebra, where he could not associate images with concepts.

New math failed because it was too abstract for the early grades. The inappropriateness of draining arithmetic of its sensory content is most obvious in young children operating at a concrete sensory level. I would argue that this approach is detrimental at the high school and college levels as well. Emptying ideas of their sensuality does not produce meaningful learning or discovery, as some of its proponents maintained, but mechanical and arbitrary learning. What must be criticized is not abstraction itself, which is too much a part of the human mind to be discarded, but abstraction at the expense of the senses rather than in conjunction with them. The present disharmony among new-math advocates makes it difficult to speak with certainty about its current status. The trend today is for a retrenchment in the curriculum. The intention of this chapter is not to heap further abuse on those already fallen but to draw the implication of the new-math controversy so that the mistakes it made will not be repeated in other fields, or again in mathematics.

The outlines of a similar controversy now brewing are seen in an article, "Why Jessie Hates English," by author Sloan Wilson. As a former English teacher from a family of English teachers, Wilson was appalled to find his daughter disliking English. The explanation, he found, was not the teacher or the school but the emphasis on a science of grammar detached from speaking and writing. The students learned rules and principles using clauses, participles, and various jargon phrases that broke language into laws and pseudo-mathematical rights and wrongs. In a properly run English composition class, Sloan argues, grammar has specific applications in reading and writing and should not be taught as a science. It should be subordinate to the basic urge to communicate and not an end in itself, except perhaps for those few advanced researchers whose special field is grammar itself.[11]

The issue here is very similar to that in the new math. It involves the *abstractification* (an ugly word for an ugly process) of material to be presented to children. It takes a subject rich in sensory content—and behind every word was originally an image—and turns it into a categorical system. This amounts to teaching English as a foreign language, which might make sense if foreign-language instruction in the United States had a record of tremendous achievement. Sadly, the reverse is true. It is generally conceded that American schools do a very poor job of teaching foreign languages. Matched against students in Sweden or Germany or France, the proficiency of American students in second languages is pitiful, and in third languages nil. This is true even in portions of the United States that border on Mexico and French-speaking Canada. I understand the historical, geographical, and ideological roots of this. But the sad state of foreign-language instruction in the United States should give one pause before making it a model for teaching other subjects, particularly English. A second language is likely to be learned arbitrarily, like algebra, without the visionary qualities required for poetry.[12] As anyone who has studied another tongue in an American school can attest, this sort of teaching reduces words to arbitrary connections and rules. John Ciardi remarked that no poet has ever written memorably in a second language. Prose, yes; poetry, no.

Biologist Farley Mowat, a naturalist at heart, was puzzled by the lack of interest many of his colleagues showed in living creatures. "Being a literal fellow," Mowat admitted, "I took the word *biology*—which means the study of life—at its face value. I was sorely puzzled by the paradox that many of my contemporaries tended to shy as far away from living things as they could, and chose to restrict themselves instead to the aseptic atmosphere of laboratories where they used dead—often very dead—animal material as their subject matter." There was even a tendency to avoid working with animals at all, even dead ones. "The new biologists," he writes, "were concentrating on statistical and analytical research, whereby the raw material of life became no more than fodder for the nourishment of calculating machines." [13] Mowat did not take kindly to a biology so detached from its presumed subject matter and spent as much time as he could studying wolves, deer, and other species in the wild.

If we do not consider directly the proper role of the senses in learning, we are going to find more articles with titles like "Why Billy Dislikes Geography," "My Ethelbert Hates History," and "Why Leonard Can't Draw or Sing." History should be a rich, vibrant subject, full of movement and mystery, not a dead recitation of names, places, battles, and treaties. Geography can be a tremendously exciting subject when it is taught in relation to the land, the water, the wind, and the labor of our ancestors over the millennia. The imagery behind the concepts must be preserved if geography—or any other topic—is to be a sensible subject.

Back to Beansticks

Mathematics educator Lloyd Scott follows Piaget's notions of mental stages. He believes that young children respond best to material that is tangible and pictorial. Rather than encouraging inhibition of children's use of imagery, Scott recommends that children should be using imagery in learning mathematics. The materials employed in teaching about numbers should therefore be of the real world. He rejects the devaluation of practical application in the new-math curriculum and the implication that examples based on buying a loaf of bread and computing the cost of an automobile are somehow demeaning. Scott is one of the few mathematics educators familiar with imagery research. He has constructed a graph showing the percentage of pictorial/tangible material to be included in math teaching through the grades. The curve runs from 100 percent in kindergarten to 60 percent in grade five, down to 10 percent in the last year of high school.[14]

The Nuffield Mathematics Teaching Project, developed in the 1960s in England, is also based on Piaget's concepts of children's developmental stages. The method emphasizes a child's experiences in manipulating materials and is individualized for each child, since it is recognized that children at the same chronological age may be at different developmental stages.[15]

The Cuisinaire method uses colored rods, from 1 to 10 centimeters in length, to teach arithmetic. It attempts to capitalize on the child's interest in sensory-motor activities. The colored rods and their numerical values are as follows: *red family:* vermilion (2), crimson (4), brown (8); *blue family:* light green (3), dark green (6), and blue (9); *yellow family:* yellow (5), orange (10); and then there are *black* (7) and *white* (1). Rather than memorizing arithmetic tables blindly, by using the rods the child can perceive relationships in their totality; that is, that two light green rods (3 centimeters each) are equal to one dark green rod (6 centimeters). The monotonous aspects of counting are replaced with active experimentation. Numbers and their relationships are visible and tangible. Three-dimensional figures can be built out of the rods, and these can be used to find area and volume in later applications of the method.

The teacher tries throughout to develop the appropriate concepts that will remain when the rods are absent. As the teaching progresses, efforts are made to wean the child away from the rods, lest too great a dependence develop. The color crimson has only an arbitrary relationship to the numeral 4 or four milk bottles. In that sense, the Cuisinaire system also relies on arbitrary connections to teach arithmetic. However, the basis of the system is sensory and perceptual, encouraging the child to see patterns, groupings, and totalities and to grasp them visually and motorically. The teacher tries to develop the child's intellectual awareness of what has been seen and built, and of how this can be applied in the real world. Frequently the children are asked to shut their eyes and mentally construct larger figures using the colored rods: "Imagine a crimson rod put on top of a white rod. Then mentally try to match this with the other color rods and see which one is the same length." Because the rods have tangible physical qualities, as well as colors to make them distinct in the child's mind, such computations can be done in the imagination as well as with the wooden sticks.[16]

Asking students to close their eyes and create mental images in response to verbal statements made by the teacher makes the students aware that imagery is connected with the rest of their experience and can be used to solve problems. The visual and the verbal learning systems are thereby complementary and interdependent. Caleb Gattegno, who has done most to train teachers in the use of the Cuisinaire system, provides numerous examples of how imagery can be used to teach mathematical properties. A teacher might verbally describe how two drops of water striking the surface of a bucket at the same time will generate two families of concentric circles. Together the students and the teacher can explore, through imagery alone, the mathematical properties of the moving circles. It is possible to draw the same example on the blackboard or show it on film, but the use of imagery exercises the child's mental faculties for visual thinking and minimizes the schism between the inner and the outer worlds. Once we deliberately begin to employ images, Gattegno declares, we obtain an awareness that imagery is one of the powers of the mind and can yield in a short time vast amounts of insights into fields that become almost sterile when the dynamics are drained from them.[17]

Balances, beansticks, and other manipulable objects are used to make numbers more tangible, more real. Instead of attempting to dissolve the child's concrete images of numbers as the new math did, these systems work with the child's capacity for sensory think-

ing and capitalize upon it. The esthetic and motor pleasure to be
had from making a scale balance through subtraction and the physical enjoyment of working with shiny beans glued to popsicle sticks
add greatly to the dimensionality of numbers. Such materials can
often be created by the children and the teacher, thereby reducing
the alienation that occurs when all the materials are supplied by
anonymous outside agencies.

One Mode of Thinking or Two?

It is not accidental that psychologists were deeply involved in the
development of the new math. Once the abstract bent of psychologists is considered, the subordination of direct experience to detached principles in the new math becomes comprehensible. I acknowledge with regret the bias of my own profession against
sensory experience. It is not only personal bias, it is institutional
bias. On the most widely used IQ tests, an abstract answer will receive more credit than a perceptual answer. When a person is
asked, for example, in what ways a dog and a lion are alike, the
only response that earns full credit is that they are both animals. To
say that each has four legs or soft fur or can run swiftly will result
in a penalty. This attitude does little to encourage careful observation or sense exploration.

Some psychologists have described the thinking of many minority students as being more perceptual than abstract. To the extent
that IQ tests and entrance examinations penalize thinking in terms
of perceptual qualities, the net effect is institutionalized discrimination. Imagine a people living in a remote land who considered
pictorial thinking the highest mode of reasoning. Competence in the
arts and crafts would be strongly emphasized in their schools. Intelligence tests, if they were needed at all, would be scored in a direction opposite to our method. The child who answered the previous question that a dog and a lion are alike because they walk
softly would receive full credit. The child who answered that they
are both animals or mammals would receive only partial credit. The
child who answered that a mountain and a tree are alike because

they change their color with the seasons would receive full credit; the child who answered that they were parts of nature would receive only half credit. This scoring system penalizes the categorical thinker and rewards the visual thinker. I don't like this bias any more than I do the existing bias of virtually all IQ tests. The pragmatic solution is to tell children who take IQ tests that they are supposed to give abstract answers, that is, to raise IQ through training in test-taking. This seems short-sighted, however, and actually reinforces the bias of the tests.

Until adolescence, there is no overall difference between boys and girls in spatial ability.[18] During early adolescence, a group difference does appear, with girls stronger in verbal abilities and boys scoring better on spatial tasks. This is affected by rate of development, since boys and girls whose physical development comes early score better on verbal than on spatial tasks, and late maturers do better on spatial than on verbal tasks.[19] If improved verbal facility is related to early maturation, and girls on the average reach physical maturity earlier than boys, this can account for their improved verbal ability during the adolescent years but cannot by itself explain it afterward. The same is true for the superior spatial ability in boys that becomes evident during adolescence and persists afterward. Either the influence of sex-typing and sex-tracking is being felt or there is something happening in the brain with regard to spatial ability. Some researchers have attempted to explain sex differences in terms of the development of different hemispheres of the brain.[20]

Like all group differences, the superior verbal ability of women and superior spatial ability of men can only be generalized to individuals with extreme caution. There will be some men who do better than most women on verbal tasks, and some women whose abilities at spatial manipulation will surpass those of most men. It is interesting to speculate on whether another sort of mathematics curriculum in grades six to eight, the period in which these differences first arise, would reduce the remoteness that many young women feel from mathematics. Much of the sex-tracking for technical occupations occurs in junior high school, when girls avoid the regular math courses required for advanced study. In the primary grades, where there is no sex difference in mathematical ability, teaching is done mostly by women. In junior high and high school, where mathematics teaching becomes a specialized activity, a larger portion of it is done by men. Rather than viewing this as a deliberate conspiracy, I look upon it as both a cause and effect of the sex difference in mathematical skills that occurs during adolescence. A likely solution is the use of alternative teaching strategies, particularly in the junior high school grades, for students with different thinking styles.

6

Super Imagers

The lamas battle hunger and cold by telling themselves
that they have feasted or that they are warm. They have
strong visual imaginations. When they make their lonely
treks through the snows to the holy places high in the
mountains wearing only a loin cloth, they don't freeze
because they concentrate on fire and warmth.

(JOHN KEEL)

A few adults and many children have images that are so bright and
clear that they are barely distinguishable from what they actually
see. This condition was called *eidetic imagery* by the German psychologist E. R. Jaensch, who believed it to be a normal quality of
childhood that was subsequently discouraged by schools which emphasized a passive approach to learning.[1] Jaensch considered such
clear visualizations intermediate experiences between sensations
and verbal memories. An *eidetiker,* Jaensch's term for someone
possessing this kind of imagery, reports *seeing* his images, in the
same sense that he would see an object in the environment. If an
eidetiker is to describe an image, he will move his eyes as if picking out specific features and display an extraordinary degree of confidence, rarely found in other people, in describing what he sees.
He will also tend to use the present tense in making his description.

The eidetic picture is often three dimensional and brighter than the object in ordinary perception, and it is seen floating "out there" rather than inside the head.

Jaensch estimated that 90 percent of children were eidetikers, but subsequent investigations employing more rigorous tests have drastically reduced this figure. Most researchers today estimate that less than 10 percent of schoolchildren are eidetic. Noneidetic young people would have clear images but would not have images with such exceptional brightness and clarity. When Ralph Haber attempted to find eidetikers in a public-school system, he had to screen some five hundred children in order to locate twenty.[2] He began his testing with afterimages. Children were asked to stare at a piece of red paper and then to transfer their gazes to a gray cardboard sheet and report what they saw. Talking about the appearance of the green afterimage accustomed the children to talking about their imagery. Following this, several illustrations from children's books were shown, and Haber made sure that the children scanned the entire picture rather than fixing their gazes on a single portion. When each picture was removed, the children were asked if they still saw an image. About one in twenty-five reported prolonged, clear images. Haber attributes the drastic reduction in eidetic images between his study and that of earlier investigations to the more detailed questions and rigorous tests he used. Many of the children in the earlier studies confused nonpictorial memory images with visual images and were attempting to come up with what the investigator wanted to hear.

Haber compared the twenty eidetic children in his sample with a matched group of noneidetikers on various tests of intelligence, achievement, and personality, but there was nothing about them that seemed distinctive other than their superior visualization. The most interesting findings concerned the ways in which the eidetic children approached tasks. Most of them required at least a three- to five-second viewing period to establish an image. Anything less than this might produce a memory, which the child could report later, but not a picture. Attempting to attach verbal labels to the details interfered with the formation of a stable image of the whole figure. This led Haber to believe that verbal memory was somewhat antag-

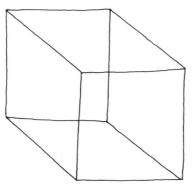

Look at this box for 15 seconds. Does it reverse? Now look away and form an image of it. Does the imagined box reverse itself?

onistic to visual memory, and vice versa. Some time after exposure to the pictures, the eidetic images seemed to break apart piece by piece until they just disappeared. They did not blur and become fuzzy, as a disappearing afterimage would. Only one of the twenty children was able to prolong an image or move it from the surface of the card upon which he was recalling the image without losing it. Nearly all reported that when they tried to move an image off the surface of the card, it "fell off and broke."

Most eidetikers are able to terminate their images at will. Sometimes they do this by blinking, looking away, switching their thoughts to something else, or shaking their heads.[3] Usually they cannot recall an image once it has disappeared, but there are some significant exceptions to this. One girl tested by Leask, Haber, and Haber claimed she could move her image anywhere, superimpose it over any object, change its size at will, choose to see it or not in the process of transition, and manipulate it by rotating it or turning it upside down.[4] Several of the children in Haber's sample said they could form three-dimensional images. This was demonstrated using a reversible cube (a line drawing of a cube that spontaneously provokes reversals in perspective) shown to the children for thirty seconds. While all twenty eidetikers reported fluctuations during the scanning period, only three experienced reversals in the mind's eye. The children were also shown a puzzle picture consisting of two ocean scenes that looked normal when seen separately, but when superimposed one on top of the other, revealed a bearded man. Only a few of the children were able to combine the two images mentally and bring the bearded man into view.

There are good imagers and then there are superimagers. Most of the children tested by Haber were good without being super. Occasionally one comes across people with such amazing capacities of recall that they seem to belong to another category. Elizabeth, a young artist at Harvard University, was carefully tested for several years by George Stromeyer, a psychologist doing research on sensory processes for Bell Telephone Laboratories.[5] It was immediately apparent to Stromeyer that Elizabeth had a prodigious memory. She could read a poem in a foreign language and years later copy it from bottom to top as fast as she could write. She could recall pictures previously seen and paint them with perfect accuracy. Stromeyer wanted to be sure that this ability was truly pictorial rather than superior verbal memory. He developed a number of ingenious tests which he felt established conclusively that she used visual thinking to reproduce the material. One test involved patterns of dots that looked random, but if viewed through a stereoscope, which presents one pattern to the right eye and a complementary pattern to the left eye, combine into a meaningful three-dimensional figure. Using only her right eye, Elizabeth was shown a ten-thousand-dot pattern for one minute. Then she was shown another ten-thousand-dot pattern with her left eye, and asked to superimpose the previous right eye pattern over it. Immediately she reported seeing the letter T moving toward her. A moderate delay did not interfere with Elizabeth's photographic memory, but after a few days the images of the complex dot patterns began to break apart. Elizabeth formed her images by inspecting one part of the scene at a time. She could not form an adequate picture without moving her eyes.

Elizabeth was able to repeat these feats with million-dot patterns, which she could retain for up to four hours. Her eidetic imagery was sufficiently strong to obscure a real percept. This was confirmed experimentally when her images of previously seen dot patterns were able to obscure actual dot patterns she was inspecting. Her images remained upright even if she tilted her head. Through her tremendous powers of visualization, Elizabeth was able to duplicate the finding of Edwin Land, the inventor of the Polaroid camera, that black-and-white photographs taken and projected through red and green filters can produce a full-color photograph with blues, yellows, and browns, as well as reds and greens. Elizabeth was first shown a black-and-white photograph of nine squares projected on the screen in red light. The next day she saw a different set of squares projected on the screen through green light and was asked to combine this with her image of the previous day's scene. She identified a full range of colored squares, including red, purple, rust, gray, green, and yellow. What she described was very close to the picture that both she and Stromeyer saw when they combined the two photographs on the screen with one projected through green light and the other through red light.

Elizabeth was subsequently tested by two investigators who were interested in monitoring her brain waves as she formed her eidetic images of pictures previously shown to her. The investigators were struck by her remarkable ability to describe a picture ''with a speed that could scarcely have been exceeded had she been looking directly at it.'' In a period of sixty-eight seconds, she supplied the following description of a Chagall painting previously shown to her:

> Horse and green man facing each other. Horse or cow. The man has a yellow hat with a red band. The horse is mostly pink and white except he is blue in the neck just above the necklace he is wearing. And under his eye is someone milking a cow. Up above this is another sort of sphere-like thing. Heading back is a green man carrying a hoe, I think, and a girl standing on her head. Behind them are houses. The one on the left is yellow. It's upright. Then there is a blue one. Then there is a red one upside down, a blue one upside down, a blue one right side up, and then a yellow one right side up. There is a moon over that. The center of the picture has a red sphere in

it. Down at the bottom center is a tree of some sort in a trian-
gular shape with some little green blobs and a bunch of brown
blobs in the branches. And the bottom left hand is mostly reds
and pinks. Bottom right there's some yellow and blue. The
sky at the top is black. Anything else?[6]

The random dot patterns were also used by psychologist Neil
Walker in a hypnosis experiment with college students.[7] Through
hypnosis, a person can be brought back to an earlier age to recall
people, places, and events that had long since disappeared from
waking memory and to employ visual cues and mechanisms in the
manner typical of earlier stages of perceptual development.[8]
Walker selected twenty student volunteers who had shown a high
susceptibility to hypnosis. He tested them three times with the
random-dot stereograms—first in normal waking conditions, second
when hypnotized but without special instructions, and finally when
brought back to age seven through hypnosis. Seven was selected as
the target age since this is when eidetic imagery is supposed to be
most intense. Each stereogram consisted of two separate patterns of
ten thousand dots that, when viewed alone, would appear as a
meaningless jumble, but when the two complementary patterns
were superimposed, a meaningful form could be seen. The stereograms showed a triangle, a T shape, and a cube with a reversible
perspective. These particular forms were chosen because they could
be described easily by young children or by someone brought back
to childhood through hypnosis.

The sequence of conditions was varied among the students.
Some saw the figures in a wakened state first, then when hypnotically regressed to childhood, then hypnotized without special instructions. Other students saw the figures first when hypnotized,
next in a waking state, then hypnotically regressed, and so on. Age
regression involved suggesting to the hypnotized subject that he or
she would become younger as the experimenter counted slowly
backward from the subject's present age back to age seven, one
year per number. The hypnotic regression was checked and verified
for all students by comparing samples of their handwriting while
regressed and awake. To reduce the possibility of bias, the labora-

tory assistant recording the replies did not know the correct response to the stereograms.

Each student looked at the first dot pattern for one minute and tried to maintain a mental image. Then he or she was shown the second part of the pattern and was asked to place the previous image over it and describe the resulting figure. Two of the students were able to identify the meaningful pattern in the combined stereogram correctly only when they were age-regressed. They were not able to do this either in the conscious waking state or under hypnosis without special instructions. Practice could not have been responsible for these results, as both students were tested in at least one of the other conditions following age regression without any success. None of the other students was able to make any sense out of the patterns in any of the conditions. Both of the successful students mentioned that as young children they were able to look at pictures and later reproduce clear images of them. One of them mentioned how she had been able to draw detailed pictures of cartoon scenes she had viewed on TV earlier in the day. Both reported the cessation of such experiences after they reached the age of ten or eleven. The ratio of two eidetikers out of twenty, or 10 percent, is similar to current estimates of eidetic imagery among American schoolchildren.

Salo Finkelstein, a calculating genius from Poland, was tested extensively by researchers in Europe and the United States in the 1930s.[9] Before audiences on several continents, Finkelstein demonstrated his amazing ability to manipulate numbers. He could memorize a five-by-five square of digits and repeat it in any sequence at a rate of about two seconds per digit. He could supply *pi* to three hundred decimal places and the logarithm of any number from 1 to 100 to seven decimal places. Finkelstein was hired by a broadcasting company to tally the returns from the 1932 Presidential election because, it was believed, he was faster than any calculating machine. Bousfield and Barry, who tested Finkelstein and attended several of his public performances, concluded that eidetic imagery was the basis of his extraordinary facility with numbers. He was also aided by kinesthetic (movement) and emotional associations. Some numbers were "nice" because they aroused pleasant associations, but other numbers were "not nice" because they were associated with things he disliked. When numbers were presented to him in yellow, a color he disliked, he showed displeasure, as if, in his words, an artistic creation had been made ridiculous. His associations included historical dates; mathematical properties such as powers, roots, and logarithms; various permutations and number series; telephone numbers of friends; and the numerical characteristics of novels such as the number of paragraphs on a page.

Bousfield and Barry wanted to discover if his images were more similar to complementary afterimages than to eidetic images. Finkelstein was asked to project images onto various surfaces that were moved toward him or away from him. A complementary afterimage, like the picture from a slide projector, gets larger as the screen is moved further away. Finkelstein's *afterimages* behaved this way and increased proportionately in size with the distance of the screen. However, his visual *images* of numbers behaved in reverse fashion. They tended to become smaller as they were projected on surfaces further away and increased in size as they were brought closer to him. The images behaved as percepts to the extent that the retinal image becomes smaller as objects are moved further away. However, Finkelstein's visual images were not perfect copies of what he had seen and heard. The numbers always appeared as if they were written on a freshly washed blackboard in his own handwriting, no matter in what form they had been presented to him. Thus he was not a classic eidetiker according to Jaensch's description.

Researchers today are beginning to doubt that anyone is a typical eidetiker any more than anyone is a typical dullard or typical genius. Intellectual abilities are so varied and complex that every individual is unique. There are *retentive visualizers* such as Elizabeth, who can recall things exactly as they were seen. There are also *inventive visualizers,* who embellish and fill out what is seen in the mind's eye. The inventive sort of visualization will be most helpful in art and design. The retentive visualizer who has total recall for material heard or read will score well on examinations testing memory. The inventive visualizer may do poorly on such examinations because the material has been embellished or altered in fantasy.

The details of a historical event may be stored in a more interesting or exciting form than the way things actually happened. That sort of imagery, which is so important in design, invention, and creative writing, is no asset on objective tests. Even some tests of visualization will test accuracy of recall rather than the creative uses of imagination.

Lightning calculators—people who are able to multiply or cube ten-digit numbers in their minds—show no need for intense concentration. Jebediah Buxton, a man of little intelligence and education, worked more slowly than most other calculating geniuses. Once he mentally squared a thirty-nine-digit number although it took him two and a half months to do it. He worked as a laborer, and the highlight of his otherwise obscure life in England was a visit from several Fellows of the Royal Society, who asked him a number of complicated mathematical questions which he was able to solve in his mind. He was able to calculate while working or talking and could solve two mathematical problems at one time without confusion.[10]

The achievements of such people depend almost entirely upon memory. They can store amounts of information very quickly. There is nothing inventive or creative in this performance. While they are not classic idiot savants—possessing one talent while being mentally retarded in everything else—most have been unable to do anything inventive or novel. It is a mistake to identify imagery, even superimagery, with creativeness. This is a stage of mental development that most superimagers never attain. Exactly why this is so, we do not know. I do not accept the explanation that their extraordinary memories prevent this. John Stuart Mill was a child prodigy who knew Greek at the age of three; philosopher and mathematical genius Pascal reportedly forgot nothing of what he had ever read; and author John Ruskin wrote excellent verse at the age of six. A prodigious memory is not automatically an impediment to creativity any more than superior imagery is an impediment to abstract reasoning. The important consideration is the degree to which the imagery is vivid, available, and controllable.

Sue d'Onim, a twenty-two-year-old college student, was known among her friends for the ability to talk backward. She could pronounce a series of words in reverse order with perfect fluency. If someone said "visualizer," she could reply, with no delay and perfect fluency, "rezilausiv." When asked how she did it, she explained that she could picture words and read off the letters in either direction. Max Coltheart and Marcia Glick tested her in the laboratory and found her limit in repeating sentences to be five or six words.[11] More than this number was difficult for her to visualize because the end of the sentence disappeared. When the investigators suggested that she divide sentences into several short rows rather than a single long row, her difficulties disappeared and she could reverse a nine-word sentence with perfect accuracy. Early in the testing, it became clear that her memory was not exceptional. Her ability to visualize material had *not* increased the amount she could remember. It turned out that she could only visualize material which she could remember independent of visualization. She had no difficulty visualizing a nine-word sentence, because she could remember it. However, she was unable to picture nine unrelated words spoken at a slow pace, since she could not remember them. Nor was she able to mentally divide a four-digit number by a two-digit number. She could not perform the intermediate operations in her mind. She was unable to solve any of the visual memory problems used with Elizabeth. Sue also did poorly on tests of spatial relations. This was confirmed in various aspects of her life. She had a very poor sense of direction and frequently became lost. Although she had lived in a town for over five years, she could not picture the area in her mind or find her way about easily. She was unable to perform choreographic tasks in ballet. She enjoyed acting but she had a difficult time memorizing her lines. She found herself forced to ad lib frequently, which was difficult to do in a production of Shakespeare.

Table 9. Spelling Words Backward

For spelling words backward, vividness of imagery is more important than control. You may not be able to do as well as Sue d'Onim, who was able to spell entire sentences backward perfectly and without hesitation, but try yourself on the following words: economical, fortification, merchandise, backward.

Based on their detailed testing, the researchers attributed Sue's capacity to talk backward to two factors. First, her ability to convert verbal memories into detailed and high-capacity visual images; and second, her ability to extract information rapidly from brief visual displays. Sue was quicker than most people in obtaining information from things seen very briefly. Her visual images were high on vividness but low on controllability. She was unable to use her images except to hold them and read them off in any direction. And she could do this only with material that she could remember verbally.

Superimager? Not in the sense that Sue could remember endless amounts of material. She was quick at forming images so long as the material was within her ken. With unfamiliar or nonsense material, she was lost. Sue d'Onim presents a mix of visual and verbal processes, some of which seem outstanding, others good, and still others fair to poor. She was not a particularly good student and did all her studying, even for courses she enjoyed, on a last-minute basis. She was an unremarkable individual except for her ability to talk backward.

Many inventors have claimed superior imagery. Nikola Tesla, the inventor of the fluorescent light, the alternating-current generator, and the Tesla coil, claimed that he could project pictures before his eyes of proposed machines which were complete in every detail in three dimensions, and he could mentally test these machines by having them run in his mind for weeks and examine the parts for wear.[12] However, none of these accounts was subject to such prolonged and careful testing as that of the young reporter who walked into the office of Russian psychologist A. R. Luria in the 1920s and asked to have his memory tested.[13] The young man struck Luria as somewhat disorganized and dull-witted, but his editor had been impressed by the young reporter's remarkable ability to remember information without taking notes. Nor did the young man, whom Luria calls S., consider that his ability was anything exceptional. S. believed that almost anyone could remember what he or she was told if there was a desire to do so. Once the testing began in earnest, Luria's initial impressions changed dramatically. There was *no limit* to how much S. could remember or how long he could retain it. Over several decades of testing, Luria found that passages S. had learned more than sixteen years previously could be recalled perfectly even when the young man had no warning that he was to be asked about the specific material. Luria eventually abandoned trying to find out how much the young man could learn and concentrated instead on the methods he used to achieve such remarkable recall.

S. would form visual images of the material he could recall at a rapid rate, reading from top to bottom, bottom to top, or in any diagonal pattern. He would pictorialize information, even when it included numbers or nonsense words. His images contained many sensory qualities other than visual patterns. Words and numbers aroused sounds, tastes, odors, and touch impressions. These cross-modality associations, or *synesthesias,* were mostly spontaneous, and they produced a blurring of the different sense modalities. There were no clear boundaries between colors and smells or between tastes and sounds. He would hear things as fuzzy and sweet, and see things as salty and wet. The meaning of words came encased in these sensations. These were not merely abstract associations, since S. claimed to hear the sounds of the number six, taste the saltiness of nine, and feel the toughness of the letter *e*. When S. described his childhood, he experienced its colors, smells, and textures.

S. employed various mnemonic devices to remember material. At first, these were rather informal learning systems. Later, when S. began giving stage performances, he improved his techniques through determined training. One device he used was the "mental walk," in which items to be learned were distributed mentally among serial locations along a familiar walk. Occasionally he found himself omitting a word in recall. His usual explanation was that he had overlooked the word because it had been left in a location that was poorly lit, out of the way, or obscured from view by something else, and he had mentally "walked on" without noticing the item. Luria felt that these omissions were more like defects of perception than defects of recall. On one occasion, S. reproduced a long series of words in which both *pencil* and *egg* were omitted. When this was called to his attention, S. explained:

> I put the image of the pencil near the fence . . . the one down the street, you know. But what happened was the image used was that of the fence and I walked right on past without noticing it. The same thing happened with the egg. I had put it against a white wall and it blended with the background. How could I possibly spot a white egg up against a white wall?[14]

When S. began giving memory performances publicly, he made his images larger and more distinct and put them in well-marked, well-lit places:

> Take the word *egg* I told you about before. It was so easy to lose sight of; now I make it a larger image, and when I lean it up against the wall of a building, I see to it that the place is lit up by having a street lamp nearby.[15]

S. developed shorthand methods for abbreviating a scene. Rather than store all of it, he would store a part that was symbolic of the whole. When an audience gave him meaningless phrases and nonsense words to recall, S. made a point of converting these into sensible pictures. He would divide a meaningless word into components and try to link them in an associated image. S. practiced several hours a day to perfect these techniques. His motivation was strong, since errors on stage were embarrassing. It was quite different from recalling things in a laboratory where everyone stood in awe of his prodigious memory. The theater audience had paid to see him perform and they expected perfect accuracy. His methods worked so well that onstage he was able to reproduce material from performances given ten years earlier without prior warning that his recall of a particular session would be tested.

Practical Utility

S. could solve intricate riddles in his head if he could imagine them in spatial terms. Puzzles about people sharing a fixed amount of money, with one person having three times as much as the other, were easy for him to visualize and work out. On rare occasions, he was able to use his powers of visualization to solve tangible problems, such as the time he proposed to a factory manager that bales of fabric could be fastened together with stretchable inner tubes rather than ropes, but such practical work was the exception rather than the rule. The main utility of his imagery lay in memorizing relevant items such as market prices when he worked for a stockbroker, names and addresses when he was a newspaper reporter, and finally items called out from the audience when he was a stage performer.

There were certain disadvantages connected with his tenacious memory. There was very little logical organization in the material he stored, and relationships between similar items would go unnoticed. Although he could learn a long list of words and reproduce it at will, if he was asked to pick out the names of birds that had appeared in the list, he would have to mentally skim over the entire list and pick them out visually. The images that were so helpful in recalling material were impediments to understanding and selecting what was essential and important. It was extraordinarily difficult for him to comprehend even a simple passage and extract the main thesis. He was so busy learning material that he did not filter it into what was important and what was not. To make such a judgment required him to retrieve the entire passage and go through it line by line as if seeing it a second time. Distractions came not only from the visual material but from the synesthesias of taste, touch, and sound accompanying all the resurrected stimuli. This was a classic case of a person seeing the trees and missing the forest. While he could recall perfectly a passage he had seen some ten years earlier, to explain its meaning would be a laborious and frustrating task.

S. complained that he had a very poor memory for faces or anything else that was changeable. He had so many different images of a person he had met under different circumstances that it was hard for him to file them away in a single category. Understanding poetry was difficult, too. When he heard a poem, his internal imagery and all the sense modalities would distract from what the poet was trying to say. Most frustrating of all was the difficulty he had forgetting anything. This was not significant early in his career, when the amount of material to be learned never challenged his capacity. But when he had to face an audience three times an evening, he found that earlier lists of words or numbers sometimes came back spontaneously as he was learning a new list. He tried numerous ways to rid himself of the unnecessary images. The only method that succeeded was for him to fixate upon the absence of the image. This breakthrough represented a tremendous increase in his control over his imagery.

In his personal life, S. tended to be verbose, distractible, and preoccupied. When asked to speak on a topic, he digressed continuously and never knew when to stop. His images also led him quickly from one topic to another. Predictably, S. did not get what he wanted out of life. He always expected to become famous. Other than recognition as a mnemonist, fame and fortune were denied him. Luria describes his life as disorganized, with dozens of job changes—each vocation merely temporary. There were times when Luria felt that S.'s imaginary world was more real for him than the people and events around him. That he died unfulfilled and is remembered only because of Luria's scholarship is not surprising. Most people lead unremarkable lives and die with their dreams unfulfilled. The most unusual aspect of S.'s life was his inability to use his impressive mental talents to make a contribution in any particular field. Had he been able to paint or compose, he might have been able to use his colored words and tasted sounds artistically. S. apparently lacked these skills. Neither did he have the engineering background to use his visualization to invent anything nor the education to be a biblical scholar.

Although eidetic images differ from ordinary images in a number of respects—such as appearing "out there" rather than in the head and being clearer and brighter than ordinary images—such perceptual anomalies are common among people who reach the top level of proficiency in any field. Professional golfers operate mentally in a very different way than ordinary golfers. The championship driver merges with the race at an unconscious level. The expert bridge player intuitively knows when to violate the rules he preaches to others. When one reaches a pinnacle of competence, one's perceptions are necessarily changed. I regard S. in much the same light as I do the others who have increased an initially high level of talent through systematic training and practice. With memory exercises (see Chapter 8), most people can improve their recall. Existing research does not reveal how high the ceiling for such memory improvement actually is. When oratory was in flower in ancient Greece and Rome, there were many people who today would be described as mnemonists—people who could recite Virgil backward or quote any line, chapter, and verse from Plato or Aristotle. Those were times when a good memory was important for professional work and for citizenship. In all probability, S. would have as difficult a time earning a living today as he did in his own time. The only hopeful thought about such people born now in the United States or western Europe is that their abilities would be detected earlier and they might be directed into careers where their gifts could be utilized.

It is important to recognize that S. was a mnemonist who happened to have extraordinarily clear imagery. In no way does this prove the necessity of imagery for good memory. Nor did S. himself process information according to the classic eidetic imagery described by Jaensch: the clear, vivid, positive image of the original scene. Instead, he used a variety of mnemonic devices, synesthesias, and bizarre associations to store and recall things. The arithmetic whiz Salo Finkelstein was able to recall long strings of numbers, but no matter how the numbers were presented to him, orally or in writing, he visualized them as if they were written on a blackboard in his own handwriting. Researchers are beginning to dispute the idea that an eidetic image resembles a photograph. It seems much more fluid and dynamic than a literal rendition, being sometimes transparent, sometimes opaque, with a few parts emerging clearly and then fading as other parts emerge.

The documentation of an extreme case is an important scientific activity. When a psychologist comes across someone with unusual abilities—extraordinary hearing, insensitivity to heat, or the ability to drink large quantities of alcohol without losing consciousness—there is value in documenting the case for a scientific audience, but in no way should this serve as a standard of comparison for the normal population. People whose abilities are unusually good or unusually poor will adopt coping strategies based on their particular situations. It is easy to confuse the primary ability with the secondary coping strategies. A good visualizer may not need to memorize material in the customary ways and may therefore neglect his powers of step-by-step memorization. A poor imager may find his powers of visualization useless for solving practical tasks and let them atrophy further.

The seeming uniqueness of eidetic imagery does not hold up well under serious examination. Most eidetikers seem more like good imagers than superimagers. Imagery is more vivid and is more frequently used, relative to abstract thinking, in childhood. Whether this is because abstract thinking is less developed or because imagery is more intense is not known. It is also clear that imagery can be improved either through work that requires visualization, such as architecture, or through specific exercises. The superior imagery of designers and artists is probably due to some combination of initial inclination that attracted them to the field and to continued practice. By the time the person has reached adulthood, it is very difficult to separate the initial endowment from the level of proficiency due to practice. Often they are not separable simply because the fullest realization of talent requires training. After S. embarked upon a career as a mnemonist, he began memory drills in earnest and changed his learning strategies. This is usually the case with anyone who goes beyond ordinary levels of proficiency.

S. represents a poor advertisement for imagery. The case for increasing the amount of visual material in the school curriculum is hardly strengthened by using him as an example. S. was not successful, either in work or in his personal life. His memory tricks are impressive but unnecessary for those with access to textbooks, notebooks, libraries, and computers. The case for a greater reliance on visual thinking does not lie in memory tricks but in its value for visual problem solving and for enriching the quality of human experience. In the next chapter, we will discuss R., whose capacity for abstract thinking is as well developed as S.'s capacity for the particular. Fortunately, there is no necessity for the reader to choose between a total reliance on one mode of thinking or the other.

7

Case Study:
The Quiet World of R.

In waking life I have only once been conscious of having a true visual image. . . . Deliberate attempts to induce such images have always been unsuccessful. I am quite unable to describe the appearance of anyone I have just left, unless when with him I have verbalized a description.

(PROFESSOR G. C. DREW)

Many kinds of creative work do not require visualization. Philosophical inquiry, for instance, is likely to favor a total immersion into the abstract. When goodness is being defined in general terms, the intrusion of images of a good friend, good wine, or any other good object becomes a distraction. Writers of a psychological bent may find images irrelevant in the search for ever deeper layers of subjectivity. "I feel words more than I feel pictures," Simone de Beauvoir admitted. "I am more sensitive to words than to images."[1] Brendan Gill, the unofficial biographer of *The New Yorker,* describes his editor's attempt to draw an outline of South America: "In misery, Shawn consented; in misery, he attempted to execute his assignment. . . . Shawn's gift is words, not imagery; his South America remained a pitiable, shapeless blob."[2] Early in the century, William James routinely tested his students at Harvard University with Galton's breakfast-table questionnaire. From intelligent and articulate students, he received reports such as this:

I am unable to form in my mind's eye any visual likeness of the table whatever. After many trials, I can only get a hazy surface, with nothing on it or about it. I can see no variety in color, and no positive limitation in extent. I cannot see what I see well enough to determine its position in respect to my eye, or to endow it with any quality of size.[3]

James stressed the importance of distinguishing between visual images and memory images. Many of his students who reported no visual pictures could remember the size, shape, and color of the breakfast table and what was on it. James was led to conclude that *"some people undoubtedly have no visual images at all worthy of the name"* (italics in the original). J. Varendonck, in his book *The Psychology of Daydreams,* describes the contrast between his daydreams, which were visual, and his directed thinking, which was almost entirely nonpictorial. He traces his inability to appreciate poetry to his lack of visual imagery. (Oddly, this was the same defect about which S., the superimager, also complained.) "I possess a certain facility for speaking in public," Varendonck asserted, "but flowery speech . . . and striking analogies are out of my reach. I am unable to make much out of little. I can only say outright what is in my mind."[4]

Mental Life of a Nonimager

I first became acquainted with R. when we both worked in the same clinic. R. was intelligent and competent, although somewhat too detached to be a good clinician. He eventually drifted into research, where his abstract approach proved no hindrance. During one of our conversations, I remarked to R. that I was doing research in imagery. R. admitted that he did no pictorial thinking whatever. This seemed surprising, so I pressed him further for details. He stated that he was incapable of recalling the face or figure of anyone he knew, even of close friends or family; he heard no inner voices or music and could not recall tastes, odors, or tactile patterns; and he did not think or dream in pictures, and certainly not in color.

I had many occasions to interview R. regarding his inner life. I did not give him formal tests as such, but there seemed no reason to doubt his word considering his high degree of psychological sophistication. The portrait of his mental life was a remarkable contrast to the account of S. Unlike S. who never achieved his dreams of fame and fortune, R. was highly regarded in his field. He had accomplished more without imagery than S. had accomplished with the most impressive mnemonic skills ever recorded.

Minor details of R.'s life have been altered to protect his identity, but the essentials, as well as the accounts of his cognitive style, are accurately recorded. An essay he wrote on the topic of orientation describes his method of thinking. Unlike S., who wrote very little, R. was a prolific writer.

An Essay by R.

Orientation

Carl Asmundson got the date wrong. When I told Helen that I had an appointment with Carl on Friday, December 15, she glanced at the calendar and commented sardonically that I was wrong again. I turned to Carl's letter and saw that our meeting was indeed scheduled for Friday the 15th. I rechecked the calendar and confirmed that December 15 falls on Saturday this year. Carl must have been looking at the November page. It was satisfying to see someone else getting dates twisted; I was beginning to believe that I was the only one who did this. When I sign business papers or checks, it doesn't matter if I am off one or two days. It might if I signed million dollar contracts with tight deadlines and penalty clauses, but I don't play in that league. None of the local storekeepers is concerned that my check says October 9 instead of October 10.

I am one of the few people who can extract square roots manually. I also know that *pi* is 3.1416. Some of my friends can take *pi* to ten digits but four is my limit. I also know that I was born on September 10, but I have no idea of the hour, minute, or what day it was. I know that Christmas is December 25, and Thanksgiving appears around November 26, but I wouldn't take an oath on either date. It hasn't bothered me that the government has shifted around holidays. I have lived to see Armistice Day changed to Memorial Day, Decoration Day, and now Veterans Day, although I have a nagging suspicion that these may be two separate holidays. I have never known the date of Washington's birthday or Lincoln's birthday or anyone else's birthday except my own. My children are pretty good about dropping hints when it is time for another present. Helen's birthday occurs some time in February.* I usually have a premonition after the first of the year to ask her for the specific date. I have no idea of my first wife's birthday or the date of our marriage or divorce. Whatever scars and memories remain have lost their temporal connections.

My friend Barbara, who also cannot remember dates, got along fine until she married into a family that sends cards for everything. She suffered severe culture shock when she found that she was expected to remember every birthday, anniversary, and death day. For a while her brother-in-law helped by providing clues a couple of days before the occasion. When he graduated from high school and went off to college, she was left to her own resources and immediately forgot her in-laws' anniversary. She tried to explain that she didn't even know the *month* her own parents were married, which only confirmed her in-laws' impressions that their son had married a crazy lady.

Friends have learned to be wary of my invitations since I am invariably wrong about dates and times. This gets us into trouble on hotel and airline reservations. It may take several trips to the travel agent to untangle mistaken departure times. My most common error is to use the wrong month in my calcula-

---

* Helen's birthday is June 30th. Helen.

tions although once I used a calendar for the wrong year. If Helen double checks my calculations I rarely make a serious mistake, although I still occasionally show up for a meeting on the wrong day. I have difficulty with movie and theater schedules. I am uncertain about whether the show is to begin at 8:00, 8:15, or 8:45. In the entertainment section of the paper I overlook the critical distinction between weekday and weekend schedules or between the times of the two features or between tonight's movie and the next attraction. I don't know what the calendar manufacturers think they are doing. Some start the week with Sunday, others with Monday. The UNICEF calendar is particularly unhelpful in this regard. It begins the week with Sunday but for most of us Monday starts the week. If you write down a Tuesday appointment on the second line you end up on Monday. Tied for last place in calendar design are the arty ones with great color illustrations and tiny numerals, and the travel calendars with the days in French, Chinese, Hebrew, and every other language except English.

For a person who has only the most fragile connection with dates, I have no trouble knowing what time it is. Night or day I can usually estimate the time accurately to within ten minutes. Month in, month out I wake up promptly at 6:30 A.M. My internal clock requires a few days to adjust on a cross-country trip but then it is back on schedule. Evenings it operates in the reverse direction; by eleven I know it is time to go to bed. I don't think there is any inconsistency in being accurate about time and vague about dates. Morning, noon, and night are tied to body rhythms that mean something to me personally while dates are external and arbitrary. For my body there is not much difference between March 15 and March 16, or February 18 and February 20, but there is one hell of a difference between 5:00 A.M. and 8:00 A.M.

Directions

I learned as a child that north was at the top of the map but that isn't too helpful in a world where up is the sky. Facing a map I know my left hand is east and my right hand is west,* but applying this in a city depends upon which way I face. Several times I owned inexpensive compasses but they never worked. In New York City, east was the area on the other side of Central Park and west was the strip along the Hudson River. Nobody ever spoke about north or south but in retrospect I guess Harlem lay north and Brooklyn south and nothing mattered much beyond the boundaries of New York City.† The sun wasn't a reliable guide because you didn't see it for very long. In Missouri I found the sun to be more helpful even though it was never true east or west. Apparently it strayed on a north–south axis over the seasons. I was told to head for the basement or the southeast corner of the house in the event of a tornado. Our house lacked a basement and I never could locate the southeast corner of the house.

When I lived in Seattle I was lost all the time. Interstate 5 cuts across the city and confuses the road grid. I would be headed towards my landmark, the Space Needle, when at some point the freeway turned and I found the Needle suddenly behind me. I am amazed how other people find their way around so effortlessly. I still have difficulty recognizing my own house or the street on which I live. Half the time I drive past the house and must make a U-turn to reach the driveway. Helen keeps telling me to watch for the mailbox on the corner or the yellow house across the street, but if I could remember these things, I wouldn't have the problem of finding the house in the first place. Helen almost ended our courtship because she couldn't understand how an intelligent person could keep getting lost. She attached a Freudian explanation to my difficulty in finding her apartment. Other drivers usually assume that they are on the right road. I've never possessed this kind of confidence. I *always* assume I might be on the wrong road.‡ I have often heard people criticize the post of-

---

* N.B. Facing a map, west is on the left and east on the right.
† N.B. Staten Island lies south of Manhattan.
‡ The technical name for this confusion is *topographical aphasia*.

fice for delivering mail to the wrong address. For my part, I am amazed at how accurate the post office people are at finding poorly marked houses on obscure streets and cul-de-sacs. Given the difficulty I have in finding my own street and my own house, I dread to imagine what I would be like delivering mail in unfamiliar neighborhoods.

I have terrible problems with names. I have always regarded introductions as a waste of time since, three seconds later, my mind is completely blank for what I've heard. Of course I don't try to associate names with brands of cigarettes or days of the week. I live in dread of the day I'm ever called to identify someone in a police line-up. It might help if I used proper names more often but the risks of using the wrong name are all too apparent. What is so frustrating is that nobody else seems to have this failing. Everybody knows my name! Nobody ever calls me Bill or Harry or Wendel. I have a friend named Frank whom people frequently call Fred. It happened so often that we have made a joke out of it, and I occasionally write him "Dear Fred" letters.

Prognosis

Sometimes I think my difficulties are connected with a lack of mental imagery. I can't form a visual picture of anyone I know, nor can I "hear" their voices internally. I am an absolute failure as a mimic. My elementary school teacher required me to sit in the back row and refrain from singing. Possibly this is hereditary because my mother was tone deaf too. In church you could easily spot her location because everyone in the same pew was singing off key.* Singing in tune requires a person to accompany the words he hears internally. I don't know the words of a single poem or song, not even the "Star-Spangled Banner" and "America the Beautiful." There is a disc jockey on a local station show who seems equally inept about

---

* Barbara's husband Alan is this way too. He can go from "do" to "do" without changing the note, just increasing the volume.

names, dates, and places. He distinguishes between left and right by remembering which hand he uses to write letters to his mother. He reminisces a lot and frequently puts a baseball player on the wrong team or credits an entertainer with someone else's lines. He has a loyal audience who make it a point to correct his mistakes. They find it more interesting to hear a forgetful disc jockey than someone who comes on like an encyclopedia.

The lack of visual imagery isn't always a hindrance. I can sketch so long as things are physically present. Anything I draw from memory tends to be stiff. I can't recall what clothes Helen wore this morning. I can reconstruct the details of our conversation at breakfast but I have no auditory image of her words or picture of her sitting across the table. This frees me from a lot of unnecessary baggage. It would be distracting to think of someone and immediately confront a full color image with stereo accompaniment. At night I can consider the day's events without hearing voices jabbering at me. The absence of imagery makes for a quiet inner life, a little like living without TV. Sometimes I think of my eyes as a camera without film. The apparatus is empty inside. I can look through its lens and see what is out there and adjust the aperture to the incoming light and focus on anything I want, but there is no point in tripping the shutter. The picture will not register on anything. Or, I wonder if maybe there isn't film inside and everything is being recorded, but I lack the developer to bring it all out. I don't know.

Interviewer's Notes

In our first sessions, R. denied having any dream images. He also was unable to report the contents of his dreams upon awakening. When I requested him to make detailed notes upon awakening, he admitted that his initial opinions had been mistaken. The absence of any recall shortly after awakening, "the slate being wiped clean" as he put it, led him to believe that there hadn't been any imagery. As he began keeping notes on a bedside writing tablet, he realized that there were sights and sounds, although he denied feeling thermal, taste, or tactile qualities. To explore his imagery further, hypnosis was attempted. However, R. was a very poor hypnotic subject. He was almost completely nonsuggestible. Under the best of circumstances, he could enter only a very light trance that was easily broken. Told to imagine himself lying on a cloud in the sky, R. immediately concluded that this was impossible and returned to a full waking state.

As a child, R. daydreamed constantly. These were Walter Mitty-type dreams, about him being a famous explorer or military leader performing heroic deeds. Although lacking in sensory qualities, R. describes his fantasies as vivid and continual. It may be difficult for a visualizer to understand how a daydream can be both vivid and nonsensory. R. explained that it was like reading a story or a history book with a moving plot but, for him, no sensory arousal. It is relatively common for nonimagers to claim that their night dreams are both intense and apictorial. However, the investigation of dream imagery during sleep, such as waking the person up during periods of rapid eye movements, which tend to accompany dreaming, have shown that dreams have more sensory qualities than reach consciousness after awakening. It is interesting to reflect upon the functional significance of dream erasure. The individual whose dreams are gone will presumably wake up rested and ready for the new day. Good imagers, on the other hand, must carry with them the baggage of the previous night. The role of imagery in marking off ''morning people'' from ''afternoon people'' and ''night people'' remains to be investigated. R. was definitely a morning person.

There are some interesting similarities between R. and Luria's mnemonist, S. When I've discussed the two men with my students, they have been almost uniformly amazed that anyone could perform S.'s feats and disbelieving that the quiet world of R. was ''for real.'' Indeed, both men perceived themselves as strangers to other people and even to the planet. Both had difficulty remembering faces and appreciating poetry, but for different reasons. S., with his tremendous memory for details, perceived the trees and missed the forest. R. had no interest in the trees but could discourse readily on forest ecology or the future of the lumber industry. R. was as much the master of the abstract as S. was of the particular. Each of them was regarded as absentminded and forgetful by others, but for different reasons. Going on trips, R. would frequently forget crucial items that someone visualizing the impending journey would immediately see that he needed. S., on the other hand, appeared forgetful despite the fact that he could forget virtually nothing. The intensity and quantity of his imagery and the distracting synesthesias made him seem preoccupied and disorganized. There were so many thoughts cluttering his mind that none seemed especially important.

R. lacks any musical aptitude whatever. He cannot mimic anyone, including close friends or family. He attributes these deficits to his lack of auditory imagery. Since he is unable to internally hear anyone else, he cannot imitate their voices, and if he cannot internally hear a song, he cannot follow the tune. Even more surprising is R.'s total failure at memorization. He does not know the full text of a single poem, song, or speech. This would not be remarkable except that R. is an extremely intelligent person who was regarded as a prodigy by many of his teachers. Although he could not recall the exact words of a political speech, he could discourse at length about its meaning and significance. As an adolescent, he took many dancing lessons but failed them all. Lacking motoric and auditory imagery, he was unable to follow the rhythm. He was a complete bust on the dance floor until the mid-1960s, when solo dancing became popular. Then R. found that his stereotyped gesticulations could pass as dancing to music that lacked a recognizable beat without a partner to discover his imposture. His problems with calendar dates were partly spatial—the inability to picture the total calendar with critical marks on it—and partly a lack of sensory associations to particular days. There was not much to distinguish March 29 from March 30, nothing special on which to fasten his thoughts.

R. scrupulously avoided those things he could not do well. Although he was a productive writer, his literary skills did not include all kinds of prose. His preferred modes were analysis and commentary. He avoided descriptive prose completely. Asked to describe a place he had visited, he would guide the conversation to his feelings about the visit and the historical/political significance of what he had seen. He had a tremendous gift for converting the concrete and particular into categories. He disliked crossword puzzles, riddles, and mazes that involved the spatial abilities in which S. had excelled. He favored abstract problems and social concerns. R.'s lack of imagery made it possible for him to analyze issues dispassionately. Luria's S. could raise his body temperature by imagining himself holding an ice cube, or adapt his eyes for darkness by imagining himself in a dimly lit room, or make his heart race by imagining a frightening scene. R. could consider any of these situations with equanimity. He proceeded directly to what was important in a news report or article without tripping over sensory baggage. His bluntness and insensitivity offended many people at social gatherings.

The case of R. contradicts Professor Robert McKim's characterization of nonsensory thought as always stereotyped and conventional.[5] A purely abstract thinker can be as creative as a visual thinker, but in different ways. R. was regarded as stiff and awkward in his personal life, but so was the superimager, S. In both cases, it seems that the exclusive reliance on a single mode of thinking impoverished the mental life and detached the person from others. Little is gained by reducing the mental style of either man to a personality disposition. Personality and cognitive style are inseparably related, and one could as logically say that the personalities of S. and R. were shaped by a reliance upon a single mode of thinking as to say the reverse. Neither statement has much explanatory value. Superimagers and anoptic thinkers are not distinct personality types.

My contact with R. ceased a few years ago when we took jobs on different coasts. We occasionally correspond, but I have had no direct contact with him since. I know from seeing his published work that he continues to have a productive career. R. is a living demonstration that imagery is not critical for success in a highly abstract field. It should be realized that his choices of vocation and hobbies are not accidental. He has been able to find niches in which he can capitalize upon his strengths and ignore his weaknesses.

The imbalance in his mental life does not trouble him greatly.

Not everyone needs to know how to dance a jig, memorize the Top 50, paint from memory, or write descriptive prose—but I don't think this is the critical issue. Society has undoubtedly profited from R.'s facility with concepts, but it does not seem that a world populated by R.'s would be a very attractive or interesting place. R. himself acknowledges the impoverishment of his sensory life, but he doubts that visualization training would be worth the time, trouble, and possible disruption to his quiet world.

8
Mnemonics

I used to have trouble remembering names until I took
that Sam Carnegie course.

(JACK C. TAYLOR)

Because memory training has a much longer history than its close
relative, visualization training, we will discuss memory training
first. This should make the special features and objectives of visualization training stand out more clearly. The best-known memory
system is the mental-walk technique described earlier, which in ancient Greece and Rome enabled orators to recite long speeches with
perfect accuracy, with all details in correct order. The method involves pairing images of places with images of objects. At the outset, a person chooses a familiar building or path for "storing"
items mentally. I might try to remember the guests encountered at a
party by picturing them standing in successive locations in my
home. I would visualize Mr. Davidson coming up the stairs, Mr.
Henderson ringing the doorbell, Ms. Spencer entering the door,
Mr. and Mrs. Brown (as a unit) standing in the hall, and so on. If I
needed to call to mind the people I had met at the party, I could
take a mental stroll through my house and retrieve my imaginary
guests. The same method of storage could be used with errands or

appointments for the day. I could leave each task under symbols representing hours or half-hours.

In the sixteenth century, Guilio Camillo began construction of his famous Memory Theater, which attempted to put all the important images of his time in their proper places. Although it was never completed, the theater was intended to be a massive mnemonic containing saints, legends, virtues, and vices. Architecture and mnemonics merged in the creation of the Memory Theater. Properly proportioned in every detail to reflect eternal truths, a walk through it was intended to put a speaker's words in harmony with the cosmos.[1] Sir Francis Bacon, the eminent seventeenth-century British philosopher and scientist, designed his house at Gorhanbury as a memory theater. The windowpanes were painted with birds, plants, and animals arranged in proper zoological classifications. Bacon needed only to imagine himself walking through the house to retrieve the proper order of plant and animal species.[2]

Even earlier, some memory devices used in the Middle Ages included the tree of knowledge, whose roots and branches were identified as areas of knowledge; and the ladder of creation, whose nine steps were associated with nine academic subjects. Ascending this ladder, one eventually reached the House of Wisdom. Visual alphabets associating letters with common household objects or distinctive animal species were also in use during this period. Such systems have come down to us in the form of illustrations of alphabet letters transformed into faces or objects. Considered today as puzzles or amusing games, their early use as mnemonics has largely been forgotten. Rosary beads and knots tied with different colored strings have also been used to keep track of important dates, events, and points of philosophical and religious doctrine.[3]

Vision was the dominant sense in most but not all of the classical memory systems. It was believed that spoken words would be retained more easily if they could be associated with something seen. Roman teachers of rhetoric formulated rules for images and rules for places. For a productive mental walk, for example, an empty building is preferable to one that is occupied, where the movement and conversations would be distracting. Too much space between locations will require a longer journey and introduce many false pathways, but the area should not be so small that the objects are crowded together. It was recommended that the distance between storage places should not exceed thirty feet, since "the inner eye, like the external eye, is less powerful when you have moved the object of sight too near or too far away." [4] In learning a series of items, it may be helpful to tie a red cord around the fifth object, a white cord around the tenth, and a blue cord around the fifteenth. Thus, if only eight objects have been retrieved by the time the object with the white cord is recovered, you know that one is missing and can return to find it. Items to be learned should be meditated upon with a murmur rather than read out in a loud voice. It is preferable to do memory exercises in the evening or early morning, when there are fewer distractions.

Classical memory training fell into disfavor during the Renaissance, when books became widely available. It was no longer necessary for people to encumber their minds with facts that were now readily accessible. Mnemonics became associated with ponderous medieval scholarship, an authoritarian system of drill and memorization repugnant to the rationalist. Fortunately the mental-walk technique survived in various forms and, because of its demonstrated effectiveness, has been "rediscovered" numerous times. Here is an account by a young man who learned the technique as a child:

> I remember when I was a kid going places in the car with my family. We played this game of remembering words by associating them with certain places along the way. We would work through the alphabet on the way to some place, and on the way home we would see who could get the most words right. . . . When I used to get bored in school I would daydream a lot. I wasn't doing too well until I started playing the alphabet game in class while the teacher was talking. I just started associating places and events in my daydreams with different things the teacher was saying. It was a lot easier to remember my daydreams than what she was talking about, so when I had to remember what I had been "taught," I just remembered my daydreams. After a while I lost track of my

In the mental walk, items to be learned are pictured and placed in sequence along a familiar path.

dreams, but they lasted long enough to get me through the test.

The effectiveness of the mental-walk technique in improving recall has been demonstrated by Bower and others in the psychological laboratory.[5] Anthropologists have provided an account of a similar technique used by the Arunta tribe of Australia, who had the ability to repeat long folk tales with impressive accuracy. It was found that the Arunta associated various parts of the landscape and details of the countryside with tribal myths. Telling a story was a matter of taking a mental walk through the countryside.[6]

Pegwords

The mental-walk technique is only one of many mnemonic aids developed since memory training first began in Egypt some 2,500 years ago. In 1648, Stanislaus von Winckelmann developed a letter code for numbers. Each digit corresponded to a consonant, and these were joined into words to learn number series. The great mnemonist von Feinaigle improved upon this system and gave stage performances throughout Europe. Systems differ in their specifics, but the basic translation goes something like this:

Digit	Consonant
1	t
2	n
3	m
4	r
5	l
6	j, sh or a soft g
7	k, hard ch, or a hard g
8	f
9	p
0	z

A mnemonic is used to aid the student in learning these consonants. The letter *t* has one vertical downstroke, the letter *n* has two vertical downstrokes, *m* has three, while *r* is the fourth letter of the word *four,* and *one* is the Roman numeral for 50, *j* is a little like a backward 6, and so on. Vowels are not associated with particular numbers, so they can be used to connect the consonants into meaningful words that can then be pictured. The person tries to visualize objects whose names include key consonants. Someone who wanted to remember my house number (322) might picture *manna* from heaven or the Spanish *mañana*. The specific images should fit the person's own interests. Some people prefer ridiculous images, some don't. I personally don't like images involving violence, even though they may be especially vivid. Several studies have found that it takes more time to form ridiculous images, and there is no improvement in recall over more mundane images.[7] Psychologist R. J. Senter employs an additional mnemonic in his list of code words by using a consistent first letter for each ten numbers.[8] The code words for 1–9 all begin with *h,* which has no numerical value, and end with the appropriate pegword sound, i.e., 1–hat, 2–hen, 3–ham . . . and for numbers 10–19, all words begin with *t* and end with the appropriate consonant sound (10–toes, 11–tot, 12–tin . . .). As in all memory systems involving visual imagery, the translations frequently involve poetic license. They are *not* literal. This is more a phonetic language than a mathematical code. Senter's pegword for 18, which in his system begins with *t* and ends with an *f* sound, is not *tiff* or *tough* but *taffy,* which he finds easier to visualize. To go back to the party example, the first person met is imagined wearing a large, green *hat;* the second is walking alongside a big, red *hen;* the third is eating a ham; the eighteenth is covered with *taffy;* and so on. A person unable to create, combine, and retrieve images has a difficult time using this system.

Learning the Canadian Provinces Using Pegwords

Go over the following ditty, each time forming an image of the pegword (*sun, glue, tree,* etc.). The more sensory qualities to the image (the warmth of the sun on your face and the bright visual image; the stickiness of the glue, its distinct odor), the better.

The following list of ten Canadian provinces goes from east to west. Read over the list several times, each time forming a visual image connecting the province name and the appropriate pegword. Don't be concerned if the image is unusual or factually incorrect; what is important is its distinctiveness and clarity. For example, you might visualize sunny Newfoundland, sticky Nova Scotia, or Prince Edward Island covered with leaves fallen from its many trees, and so on.

> Newfoundland
> Nova Scotia
> Prince Edward Island
> New Brunswick
> Quebec
> Ontario
> Manitoba
> Saskatchewan
> Alberta
> British Columbia

In past centuries, there have been various number systems based on visual images of objects resembling digits. The number 1 would be pictured as a candle or a tall tree, 2 as a swan, 3 as a trident or pitchfork with three tines, 4 as a cube, and so on. Later variations of this technique were less dependent upon visual likeness of the digits than to a verbal rhyme. The person starts out learning a ditty, "One is a bun, two is a shoe, three is a pea, four is the floor. . . ." The exact pegwords are not important so long as they are easily pictured and rhyme with numbers. Like the list of familiar places in the mental-walk technique, once this rhyme has been learned, it can be used over and over. The person associates the visual image for each pegword with the items to be learned. If one has to remember a list of things to do around the house—mow the

One is the sun

Two is glue

Three is a tree

Four is an apple core

Five is a beehive

Six is sticks

Seven is in heaven

Eight is a plate

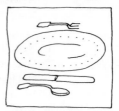

Nine is brine

Ten is a hen

lawn, water the flowers, put the roast in the oven, phone the dentist for an appointment, and so on, one might visualize a lawn mower chewing up a large bun, flowers growing out of a shoe, the roast in a green oven shaped like a gigantic pea, and the dentist sliding along a polished floor. As soon as one retrieves the image, one knows immediately the numerical position of the item in the series (the object with the large pea is number three, and whatever floats in heaven is number seven). Students asked to memorize lists using a pegword system do much better than students left to their own devices. They also are vastly superior in recalling the correct serial order.[9]

Current memory systems tend to make few demands upon the visualizing capacity of the learner. This is realistic in terms of the widespread atrophy in sensory thinking, but it also contributes to that decline. Typical of the verbal mnemonic systems is Victor Werner's book *Shortcut Memory*.[10] Upon being introduced to "Mr. Haffner," Werner recommends that the listener immediately form *assimilations* or similar-sounding words such as half-hear, half-near, or half-nerve, which are then associated to some distinctive feature of the person's face. Some of the similar-sounding words undoubtedly have visual qualities, but others are almost entirely abstract, such as "claims one" for Clements. Werner ends his book with a dictionary of code words for numbers. For example, *044* would be *sorority, soarer, swearer,* or *sorrier,* and *511* would be *allotted, hold-out, wielded, yielded,* and several other polysyllabic words with *l*s and *d*s. This system has considerable appeal to word-dependent individuals. The mnemonic devices used by my students in their college classes are almost entirely verbal. In addition to the ubiquitous "Thirty days hath September, April, June, and November . . ." and *"i* before *e,* except after *c* . . ." and "In 1492 Columbus sailed the ocean blue," their favorites include:

"King Phillip Came Over from Germany Stoned," used in zoology
    to remember kingdom, phylum, class, order, genus, and species.
"IRAC," law-school mnemonic for issue, rule, application, and
    conclusion.

"The Stamen is the Anther to the Pistel's dreams," to remember flower reproductive structures in botany.

"Never Lower Tilly's Pants, Grandma May Come Home, First Letter of Bone," medical-school mnemonic for the bones of the hand (medical students have many bawdy mnemonics for use in anatomy classes).

The knuckle method of remembering months with thirty-one days: counting across the knuckles to find the months with thirty-one days, the spaces in between are the months with fewer days.

"How I wish I could recollect of circle round, the exact relation Archimede unwound." (The digits of *pi,* 3.141592 . . . are identified by the number of letters in each word).

"Put Eggs On My Plate, Please," for learning the different eras.

The first letters of the names of the Great Lakes spell *HOMES.*

LEJSAS, the first letters of the seven articles of the Constitution.

My teenagers knew many of these and added a few more, including "Kings Play Chess on Fine-Grained Sand" (kingdom, phylum, class . . .). A biology teacher had taught this to my older boy, who then taught it to his younger brother. My daughter came up with NAPCAVIP (noun, adjective, pronoun, conjunction . . .).

"Roy G. Biv," the order of spectral colors.

The order of the planets from closest to farthest away can be re-remembered by "My Very Educated Mother Just Saved Us Nine Pizzas."

Since most of these devices consist of fewer than ten words, they are probably used more for learning sequence than learning the individual items. Ordinary memorization would probably be sufficient for the names of planets or spectral colors, but the mnemonic tells the order. Almost without exception, these are verbal devices rather than visual. They work because they are cute, distinctive, or form a rhyme or an acronym. If there are too many of them, there will be problems knowing which is the correct mnemonic. Anthropology students must remember whether it is the dog with fleas, King Phillip, or eggs, since the association between time periods and the jingle is purely arbitrary. It would be in the students' interest to form a visual bridge between ancient time periods and putting eggs on the plate. A dinosaur egg would probably do the trick, or a miniature dinosaur standing on scrambled eggs. A visual image of a hand pulling down Tillie's pants would probably help the anatomy student remember that this mnemonic concerns the bones of the hand and not the foot or the skull. The predominance of verbal mnemonics is another indication of the decline of imagery in the classroom.

One must beware of ditties that create incorrect stereotypes. Consider a mnemonic for a class in abnormal psychology—Six Campers Packed Heavily—for learning the four varieties of schizophrenia (simple, catatonic, paranoid, and hebephrenic), with the student visualizing six campers full of crazy people. This is not an image of schizophrenia I want students to have. How about Sad People, Helpful Clinic? That seems more like it, but not all mental patients are sad (some are irrepressibly joyous) and not all benefit from psychotherapy. It seems irresponsible to ask students to form images so simplistic and incorrect. As a psychologist who has studied both perception and learning, I cannot help but believe that converting Mr. Murphy to Murder-For-a-Fee will affect my attitude toward him, even at an unconscious level.

Harry Who?

Often described as the world's number one memory expert, Harry Lorayne has written several popular books and given numerous stage demonstrations of his mnemonic prowess. He has numerous testimonials from people, both famous and ordinary, as to the effectiveness of his system. My own experience with it and that of my students is that it works. The basic rule is to transform ideas to be remembered (names, places, or numbers) into "picturable equivalents," which are then linked together in "ridiculous associations." It is a step-by-step process even though it proceeds at a rapid pace. Upon being introduced to someone, one immediately transforms the person's name into a visual image related to its sound or meaning. (Dougherty becomes *do hurt T* or someone kicking a golf tee, and McHenry becomes a Mack truck with a single hen inside.) The more unusual the image, the better. The image is then associated with a distinctive feature of the person's face—the Mack truck driving out of McHenry's bushy eyebrow and the broken golf tee located on Dougherty's flat nose. This connects name with face. Additional associations of job, rank, title, or birthday are formed in the same stepwise fashion. If Dougherty is a vice president, a vise closes around his nose in which the golf tee is embeded.

Practice in using the technique leads to proficiency. Lorayne encourages his pupils to select in advance picturable equivalents for names and titles frequently encountered, just as a practitioner of the mental walk selects in advance familiar storage places. A company president might be pictured as a printing press, a treasurer as a dollar bill, an accountant as a ledger, a general as a star, and a lieutenant as a lute. Lorayne's book on remembering people lists picturable equivalents for eight hundred common American surnames.[11] Having these images "on file" saves time and trouble when meeting new people. For names not included in the list, an extensive vocabulary and poetic license are helpful.

Since the system is based on visualization, it is no surprise that Lorayne thinks visually and believes that other people have this capacity. His claim, "You can't think without seeing pictures," is similar to that made by Aristotle many centuries earlier. How often people actually do think in pictures seems a less important issue than whether the capacity can be developed through practice. Lorayne's career provides a clue to what Luria's S. might have become if he were living today in the United States. A few performances on the Jack Paar and Johnny Carson shows would have guaranteed S. bookings on the lecture circuit and advance royalties on a future book and perhaps offers from Las Vegas. The extent to which this would have changed his private life as distinct from his public image is difficult to say. S probably would have needed some editorial help in writing his book and in making the financial and travel arrangements for his lecture tour, but that is what agents and editors are for. As individuals, S. and Lorayne are very different people. Lorayne seems an outgoing, practical person who enjoys meeting people and helping them improve their memories, while S. was reclusive and impractical. This indicates the fallacy of believing that mnemonists have much in common other than their style of thinking. A business relationship or marriage between a visualizer and a verbalizer may succeed because the complementarity expands each person's capabilities. What is important is that each person should know how the partner thinks.

What's a Good Memory Worth?

The Shass Pollak were Jewish memory experts whose special feats were limited to the Talmud. *Shass* is the Hebrew word for a portion of the Talmud and *Pollak* means Pole in Yiddish. A Shass Pollak was therefore a Pole who knew thousands of pages of the Talmud by heart and could demonstrate his powers on request. Accounts from reliable informants of several such performances were collected by George Stratton.[12] To understand the memory feat, one must realize that the Babylonian Talmud consists of twelve large volumes amounting to thousands of pages of text, and all printed editions of this version contain the identical number of pages and the same word order on each page. A performance by a Shass Pollak would go something like this: Someone would open any volume of the Talmud to any page and select a specific word, for example, the ninth word on line twenty. A pin would then be pressed into the word until it went down thirty or forty pages. The Shass Pollak would be able to state the word found at that exact location (word 9, line 20) on the next thirty pages. Witnessing such a performance, Dr. Schechter, the president of the Jewish Theological Seminary of America, was surprised to find that the man knew little of the content, meaning, or application of what he had memorized. Not one of the Shass Pollak, as far as he knew, had become a distinguished scholar or scientist. When Schechter suggested to the man that he use his skills in the service of humanity in some literary or scientific capacity, the Shass Pollak reacted to the statement as nonsensical. In a society where the Talmud is readily available, one must admit there would not be much practical value in having someone who knew it by heart but did not understand it. In ancient times, however, the Talmud was passed on solely by memory. The Shass Pollak were the vestiges of a practice that had been vital to the cultural survival of the Jewish religion.

This account of the Shass Pollak was written by George Stratton in 1917. Unlike most psychologists of his day, Stratton took seriously people's reports of their own experiences (he was subsequently to become famous for his experiments involving wearing special glasses that turned the world upside down). He did not, as far as I know, ever test a Shass Pollak personally. Apparently he saw no need to do so, since a number of trustworthy observers had done this for him. What is lacking is a description of the methods used to train the Shass Pollak. As in the case of S., it seems more likely that superproficiency is the result of initial talent and intensive training. Many of the best-known mnemonists were educated in eastern European schools where memory drill was a daily routine. If we are to do more than treat mnemonists as curiosities, we must ask whether there would be any value today in someone memorizing the New Testament, *Webster's Dictionary,* or the entire *Encyclopaedia Britannica.* The variety of editions, revisions, and type faces would preclude achievements similar to those of the Shass Pollak. But would there be any practical value in someone memorizing any of these books without understanding the contents? The honest answer is probably no. Other than the notoriety it might bring, it would have little or no practical value.

This is not the case in places where the oral tradition remains alive. When he was searching for traces of his slave ancestor, Kunta Kinte, *Roots* author Alex Haley describes how he went to a back-country village to find the old men, called *griots,* who were trained to be "living, walking archives of oral history; some could relate their villages' histories for three days without repeating themselves." Haley listened to the *griot* whose specialty was the Kinte band. The man went on for hours, reciting family history. Then suddenly the old man reached the year (1767) when "the King's soldiers came. The eldest of these four sons, Kunta, went away from his village to chop wood . . . and he was never seen again." Haley's story moves from Africa to Annapolis, Maryland, where the slave ship *Lord Ligonier* landed. From then on, there was no single person who retained the oral history of Haley's family. During his years of intense research in over fifty libraries and archives, Haley became a historian in the contemporary mode, not a *griot*. [13]

In the imagination of science-fiction writers, things have gone in the opposite direction—from books to no books. The film *Fahrenheit 451* shows a brutal new culture overturning the old culture and burning all its books. Survivors from the old culture huddle together in small bands outside the cities, and each person has the responsibility of memorizing a book. In this kind of situation, it would be helpful to have someone in the group who had memorized the entire *Encyclopaedia Britannica* or an unabridged dictionary. But even accepting the remote possibility of such a situation, it would probably be more practical for the survivors to secure copies of important books, bury them in a time capsule, and remember its location than to carry around volumes in their minds.

One does not have to look to science fiction to establish the value of a good memory in business and personal life. People like to be remembered by name. The salesman who calls Bill, Jack, or vice versa, or the host who introduces a guest using the wrong name, will leave a bad impression. The benefits are not solely confined to the business world. A common complaint among university students is that "nobody knows my name." When the student is about to graduate and needs letters of recommendation, this is a serious predicament. In large classes, students don't even know one another by name. Sitting in long rows in a lecture hall facing the front of the room is not conducive to informal conversation. Every semester students will come to my office and ask minor questions that any of their fellow students could have easily answered—except for the fact, they explain apologetically, that they don't know any other students, even people they have been sitting next to for eight weeks. The university professor who knows his or her students by name or who can help them know one another will reduce such feelings of alienation.

There is a chemistry professor on my campus who memorizes the names and faces of all two hundred students in his class. He does this at the beginning of every quarter, using photographs. It usually takes him about three weeks of practice to connect the names and the faces. "I look at the pictures while I am eating, shaving, and just before I go to bed," he explains, "as well as in the laboratory, where I practice associating the names with the individual students." He does this to overcome the impersonality and anonymity of his large class. Students appreciate being called on by name and it keeps them alert. What sets this instructor apart from most of his colleagues is less his mnemonic prowess than his active commitment to knowing his students by name.

The value of a good memory is evident in any large organization. I remember how much pride factory workers felt when a front-office person called them by name. This was a sign that you were known and had some prospect for advancement. The boss was unlikely to promote people he didn't know by name. This may be less true today in large factories and offices where promotions and raises are done through seniority and contract regulations, but personal contact still plays a role in middle-sized companies. Compartmentalization is also a serious problem. The left hand not only doesn't know what the right hand is doing, it frequently doesn't even know that there is a right hand. Christmas parties or retirement dinners may bring employees together, but even on such occasions, people tend to remain close to those they already know. The situation is even worse when offices are located on different floors in a high-rise building. A person may not be acquainted with anyone on the floors immediately above or below or know what activities go on there. Helping people connect names and faces seems likely to improve communication, reduce isolation, and raise morale. Even if this does not dramatically raise production, the benefits of memory training seem worth the effort. Perhaps the critical factor would not be the exercises themselves but the interest of management in better human relationships and the interaction (by name) in the memory classes. All this is part of the mnemonic package.

It is, however, shortsighted to think of memory only in productivity terms. The case for memory, and more specifically for pictorial memory, is related more to the quality of experience than to party tricks or added income. People who can enjoy their sensory imaginations are not so dependent upon advertiser-dominated media for their images—they can revive their own and develop new ones. When I was a child, my mother wanted me to get as much experience as I could because, she solemnly declared, no one could take it away from me. She assumed that the fullness of experience would always remain with me. To store visits of places visited or of the people I met under verbal labels without any sensory reverberations was not what she had in mind.

Teaching Mnemonics in the Schools

Mnemonic systems have been in existence for over 2,500 years. Their effectiveness has been established not only by their survival but by laboratory experiments. Gordon Bower, one of the most active researchers in this field, believes that some of the difference between smart pupils and dull pupils lies in their learning strategies. A smart kid knows how to remember things and a dull kid doesn't. Since efficient learning strategies can be taught, there seems no reason why the gap between slow and fast learners cannot be reduced. Bower cites a study in which ordinarily large differences in learning between normal and retarded children were nearly eliminated when both groups employed an imagery approach.[14]

The reason these systems are not applied in the schools has little to do with their effectiveness. It is primarily a matter of a model muddle centering about the goals of education. The Renaissance produced a strong reaction against memorization that persists to this day. Mention memorization to an educator and you are likely to get a shudder and a look of dismay. There is some hypocrisy in this attitude, in view of the large amount of memorization required on examinations in which students must list the names of state capitals, the Great Lakes, major battles, the planets in order of distance from the earth, various animal and plant species, and so on.

Unfortunately, the ideological opposition of educators to memorization prevents them from teaching students better recall methods. Psychologist George Miller's boyhood teacher told him that memory crutches were only one grade better than cheating and Miller would never understand anything properly if he resorted to such underhanded tricks.[15] This did not stop Miller and other students from using mnemonics; it only made them conceal their method of learning.

Memory training has been banished from the classroom. Visual imagery, having been associated with mnemonics for several thousand years, did not escape the prejudices against mnemonics. Psychologist Ian Hunter considers mnemonic devices to be a second-rate and childish method of learning material, the same criticism directed against imagery in the classroom. Hunter believes mnemonics to be useless in most all practical situations. When applied by Harry Lorayne or some other stage performer, he believes it is an exhibition piece that is spectacular but not otherwise useful in the ordinary business of life.[16] This overlooks the importance of memorization in almost all educational institutions. Teachers define their objectives in more general terms, such as getting students to read, write, add, and possess various technical, social, and artistic skills, but the success of their efforts is measured largely through tests of memory. Knowledge of a subject is gauged by how well the student can recall the correct answer. This is not a matter of creatively solving a new problem but of recalling the correct information or formula. A perusal of examinations used at all grade levels reveals the importance of memory. Teachers may believe that they are teaching students how to think, but they are really testing what students can remember.

When the implications of this inconsistency are considered within the educational establishment, several alternatives appear. One possibility is to reduce the amount of recall required in examinations. The student would no longer be required to learn state capitals, the names of famous explorers, or the definitions of adverbs and conjunctions. This would compel teachers to test the students' ability to apply knowledge in a new situation rather than regurgitation. Students would be asked to solve certain arithmetic problems or write proper sentences, or to consider international disputes in historical terms. The emphasis would be upon solutions rather than recall. Yet it should be obvious that application is a two-step affair, and the first step requires memory. The student has to recall the correct procedure and/or information before applying it. Rather than eliminating the need for recall, tests of problem solving go one step further. Memorization is the hidden agenda of the classroom. Until this is recognized, there is not going to be any serious attention paid to memory training.

Questions about who should undertake instruction in mnemonics, and when, where, and how it should be done can be solved largely on a technical level. Obviously those who conduct memory-training sessions should know something about it themselves. This could be accomplished through some combination of workshops, summer courses, and extension programs. Mnemonics need not be taught at the expense of other subjects. If pupils were able to develop more efficient learning strategies, the savings in all courses would be tremendous.

It must be stressed that there is no single best method of memory training. The mental-walk technique seems best suited for students who are visual-minded, while students who are more verbal-minded would probably find the pegword system more congenial. One does not have to accept the initial level of visualization as indicative of potential. Just as verbal memory can be improved through memory training, visual memory can be improved through visualization training (see Chapter 9). Knowing the history of mnemonics and its current position of low regard in the educational system should help clarify parallel developments in visualization training and also the obstacles against its acceptance in the schools. The need is not for special courses in visualization training in the early grades but to encourage teachers to leave the child's capacity to visualize intact.

9
Visualization Training

I don't play an instrument and I don't sing. It might be
that I don't sing because I can't recall how a tune goes and
it would be hard to sing in such a situation. A lot of my
friends sing well and they say it's because they can hear
the music inside their heads. I wonder if you can develop
such an ability with practice?

(COLLEGE SENIOR)

There is a virtual unanimity among imagery researchers that everyone has the capacity to think visually. This is as innate a potential
as drawing or building or the use of language, or any other skill
that develops through practice. If the potential is there, there is the
possibility of improvement through training. Not all people can
become superimagers, any more than they will be able to sketch
like Leonardo or cook like Escoffier, but everyone has the potential
to improve the pungency of his or her thinking over what it pres-
ently is. Whether or not a person chooses to do this is another matter. This chapter will explore the various methods for improving
visualization.

Training can involve either vividness or control or both. The
practical value of lively fantasies while reading or listening to lec-

tures can be minimal and in some cases negative. Misunderstandings between people and personal difficulties connected with imagery may be due to a lack of control rather than clarity. The child who is told by teacher or parent to ''stop daydreaming'' may not know how to turn off the interior camera. In certain types of schizophrenia, fantasy becomes the dominant reality. On the other hand, some people have developed a dictatorship of the will that does not grant images any freedom, and their thinking has a contrived and stereotyped quality. Most training tries to improve both vibrancy and control, enabling people to direct their fantasies as needed and occasionally to hold conscious control in abeyance and let the images run. As we shall see, very little has been written directly on the topic of imagery training. It is therefore necessary to begin with a detour through related topics, such as memory training.

Mnemonics Revisited

The chief connection between mnemonics and imagery training is that most memory systems rely heavily on visualization. The authors of memory books don't use the specific term *imagery* very often and instead speak about mind pictures, picturable equivalents, mental connections, and eye-mindedness. However, most mnemonic systems require the student to visualize mental connections. Bruno Furst's popular memory book is one of the few to devote a specific section to visual exercises. ''Visualize what the characters in Romeo and Juliet are doing,'' Furst encourages, ''and don't be satisfied until your mental eye sees things just as clearly as your real eye.''[1] Although Furst provides many procedures for improving verbal memory, his only suggestion for improving visualization is practice, practice, and more practice.

Although memory systems rely heavily on visualization, the reverse is not true. Visualization training avoids any hint of memorization. It also offers different rewards to a different audience. Memory training is intended to help salespeople, waiters, and teachers remember names, faces, and other useful information. Visualization training offers its students flexibility in using nonlinear thinking and an improved capacity for graphic expression. If visualization training is instrumental to any specific fields, these would be art and design. Comparing the proffered rewards to mnemonics and visualization training, the one in dollars, and the other in creativeness, it becomes clear why mnemonics is far more popular than visualization training. There are ten books on the market dealing with memory training for every one concerned with practice in imagery. Psychologist R. J. Senter observed that memory books at his local public library were perpetually out on loan and there was always a lengthy list of borrowers awaiting their return.[2] Visualization training is neglected largely because its goals do not produce tangible rewards. If proficiency in the arts were generally highly regarded in this society, the value of visual thinking would be self-evident. There is no need to tell artists and designers that visual thinking is important, or to tell musicians and composers that auralization is important. They already know this.

Imagination Training

There are many books available on creativity, brainstorming, and verbal blockbusting. Since imagery is often linked with creativeness, this seemed a promising source of material on imagery. Sadly, these hopes were not realized. As with mnemonics, imagery turned out to be a stepchild of creativity. Most exercises to develop imagination dealt strictly with *verbal* creativeness, more specifically divergent thinking. The goal was to change the direction rather than the mode of thinking. The books were verbal rather than visual, and barren of illustrations. They presented the reader with puzzles and intellectual games, but these were almost entirely verbal. Even when there was a suggestion that visualization was helpful, no exercises were provided to develop it.

Typical of imagination training is the simile problem. In separate five-minute periods, the person finds as many similes as he can for lines such as:

> As foolish as . . .
> As smooth as . . .
> As fast as . . .

Afterward the lists are examined for range and content of answers, sense modalities used, and distinctiveness of each response. Other problems ask the person to develop novel uses for common objects. How many uses can you think of for a silk hat? A pencil sharpener? The problems are again more verbal than visual. The research cited in support of these procedures comes from cognition rather than perception. They follow an exercise model of keeping fit mentally through daily practice. There is very little in them directly relevant to imagery training.

Visual cues, similar to mnemonic devices for verbal recall, will help retrieve visual information. The mnemonist S. reduced visual images to key elements in order to retain more of them. Francis Galton described the value of partial cues. The insides of a familiar house could be visualized more clearly when looking at it from the outside than by looking away from it. Chess players find the use of a blank board helpful when they play mental chess, as it is much easier to visualize moves on a blank board than without the board.[3] My own students sometimes carry notebooks and textbooks into an examination room, not to cheat, but to help trigger relevant associations. The sight of the familiar green book cover or the spiral notebook so intimately connected with lectures and studies helps locate needed passages in the mind's eye.

One reason why there are not many books on visualization training is that the eye-minded are not interested in writing books, at least the conventional sort of book—drawing a book, perhaps, or planning a book, but not writing it sentence by sentence, paragraph by paragraph, chapter by chapter. Book-writing can be likened to shoveling dirt into an enormous trench or slogging through the mud for months and years. Who would want to do this when he or she might soar above the ground on wings of fancy? This is probably another reason why there are so few written descriptions of visual or aural thinking available. In an earlier chapter, I had credited this to the tendency of people to take their styles of thinking for granted. I would add to this the reluctance of visual people to immerse themselves in the exhausting tedium of book-writing. I recognize the incongruity of writing a book about visual thinking. Many of the books on imagery, and much of the research on the topic, has been done by nonvisual types. A book such as this is necessarily linear. If it were not, it would be, as they say, disorganized and confusing. There are, however, some exceptions.

An excellent workbook for imagery training has been prepared by Kristina Hooper for England's Open University. This is an exciting venture in adult education on a national scale using radio, TV, and part-time instructors who correspond with students and grade essays and projects by mail. "Art and Environment" is an interdisciplinary course taught in the program whose Unit 5 is titled "Imaging and Visual Thinking." The workbook accompanying this section contains many valuable exercises for developing imagery. They include, besides encouragement and practice in visualization, exercises to develop clear perception in all the senses through sketching, photographing objects from different angles, touching objects, being sensitive to what is heard, smelled, and felt; practice in reconstructing the process of creating something; for example, a dress one has sewn or a bookcase one has built; and as a final exercise, interviewing other people about their imagery. Even though the approach is necessarily sequential, the book is a medley of photographs, drawings, and handwritten notes, which is about as much as one can do with visual material and still follow a lesson plan.[4]

Grace Petitclerc published an interesting teaching tool which asks a child to explore objects that she cannot see, using touch and her powers of visualization.[5] Richard de Mille uses children's games involving guided fantasies. In one game, the child is asked to imagine "a boy standing in a corner of this room . . . let us give him a hat. What color would you like the hat to be? Let us give him a jacket. What color jacket shall we give him? Now change the color

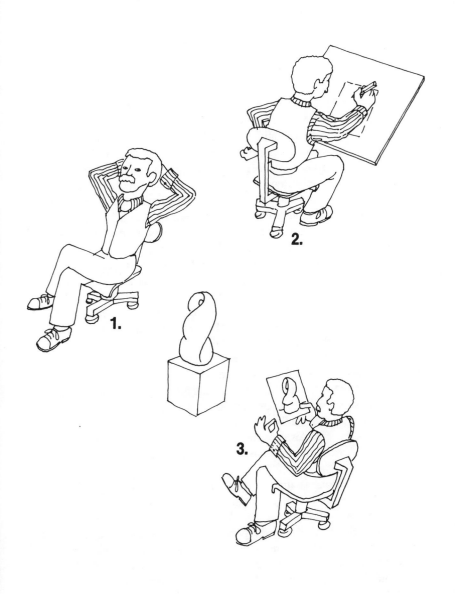

Sensory training (visual): Look, draw, compare.

of his hat. What color did you change it to? Change it again. What color this time?''[6]

By far the most comprehensive collection of imagery exercises is found in Robert McKim's excellent workbook.[7] McKim teaches a course in rapid visualization at Stanford University's School of Engineering to improve perspective drawing and visual problem solving. Since various experiments have shown that imagery improves when the person is physically inactive,[8] McKim recommends that his techniques be preceded by relaxation methods such as breathing exercises, meditation, autosuggestion, and, occasionally, hypnosis. Some writers go further in suggesting that people who are restless and hyperactive would tend to be poor imagers.[9] They are so engaged motorically that they have no time for the relaxed concentration that releases images. This is an interesting notion, but there is very little factual evidence behind it. Some of the most visual architects with whom I have worked have been extremely nervous types. I always credited this to the frenetic pace of architectural practice, where sixteen-hour workdays are not uncommon. I have never considered architects or artists, either individually or collectively, to be relaxed and easy going. However, this is not inconsistent with the notion that relaxed concentration releases imagery and tension suppresses it. There is a difference between general personality traits, which rarely are as pervasive as they sound, and transitory moods. The designer must have the ability to switch between frantic, directed activity and relaxed awareness as the situation demands.

Visualization training, as McKim teaches it, involves three related processes—seeing, imagining, and drawing. Most people do not see the world sharply and clearly. They look but miss most of what is there. McKim uses puzzles and games to improve visual recognition, such as presenting five versions of a single playing card, four containing errors and one that is correct. The solution requires the person to "really look" at the cards and notice minor errors, such as a spade upside down or *10* written as *01*. One can conceive of analogues to these puzzles in other sense modalities, such as six tones played in succession, with one of a higher pitch than the others. The same procedure could be followed with fabric or spices presented to someone who is blindfolded. The goal is to get people to pay close attention to what is before them.

The second part of McKim's system is imagination training. A person is asked to close his or her eyes and visualize a wooden cube whose sides are painted red; then to imagine two parallel, vertical cuts through the cube, dividing it into equal thirds. Then, two more vertical cuts perpendicular to the first ones, dividing the cube into equal ninths. Next, two parallel, horizontal cuts are made through the cube, dividing it into twenty-seven cubes. The person must then imagine how many cubes are red on three sides. On two sides? On one side? How many cubes are unpainted on all sides? McKim also uses two-dimensional designs which can be folded together to make three-dimensional figures (see page 65). The person tries to mentally fold a design and then indicate which of several test figures would result. More difficult problems ask the person to mentally rotate several figures at one time, such as large and small gears rotating in different directions.

The third phase involved sketching as a means of thinking schematically, which McKim calls a graphic talking to oneself. The student begins with free doodling, then proceeds to disciplined doodling, then to realistic drawing, and finally to drawing from visual memory. Later there is practice in drawing things that are felt rather than seen, such as objects hidden in a paper bag. Because of McKim's particular interest in visual thinking, most of the training involves inner and outer vision. However, it is easy to conceive of similar exercises involving the other senses. The basic principle in all these procedures is that practice accompanied by prompt feedback will improve performance.

Reporter Ross Parmenter developed techniques for improving his powers of observation. His Hunt for Similes (Fishpond Game) deserves to be classified as an imagery-training technique. Parmenter came upon this on a flight between Ottawa and New York City in order to pass the time. Whenever he spied an object, he asked himself, "What does it recall?" and made himself answer in a different material, species, or modality each time. A winding road resembled a tortoiseshell hairpin, a stream suggested worm tracks in wood, and a large bridge suggested two cranes curving their necks forward

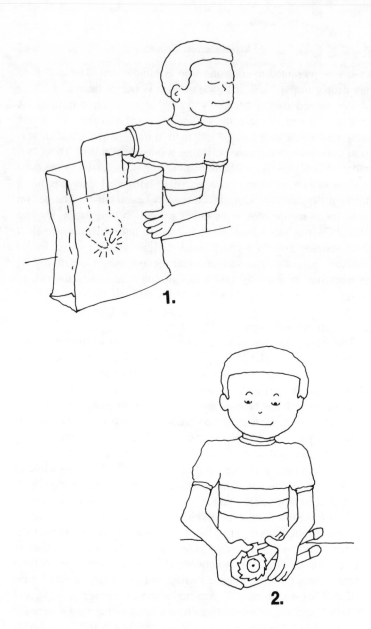

Sensory training (tactile): Feel it inside the bag, then check it out.

to kiss one another. As the game continued, the similes came more quickly. He felt that his skills as a writer in producing similes were helped by the game. These techniques involve seeing things from a fresh perspective and then converting them into words. He likens words to a developing fluid that brings out memories from a blank sheet of photographic paper. To improve powers of observation, he recommends making a conscious effort to see things as if one were a reporter on a news assignment, covering events for a local newspaper or a special-interest periodical, such as a music magazine or an aviation digest. This encourages seeing things clearly, naming things, and using details that will conjure up images for others.[10]

What is lacking for all these techniques is information on how they work. As parlor games, they are fun and harmless. However, before they are included in school curricula or mnemonics workshops, some efforts must be made to measure their effectiveness.

I have found that nonimagers can handle many of these tasks on a completely nonpictorial basis. The person deduces logically what a three-dimensional figure will look like rotated in space and formulates rules to determine which item in a series does not belong. A weak imager can name the color of a child's hat in DeMille's game without actually seeing it or feeling the material. Tasks involving creative work or movement, such as drawing or role playing, are more likely to insure the use of imagery than are strictly verbal tasks.

There seems virtual unanimity among all those who attempt visualization training that a state of deep relaxation is desirable. A college student described the problem he had writing fiction in class: "I don't get many images when I have to do it; they usually just flow when I am in a relaxed mood." As a potter described it, "I can relax, shut my eyes, and get into a state where I just see images on my eyelids as though watching a slide show." This is another difference between visualization training and memory training. Few if any of the mnemonic systems recommend relaxation; most, in fact, emphasize mental alertness.

Those people who are able to reach a deep state of meditation are also likely to produce rich and detailed visual images.[11] Good visual imagery is associated with regular breathing and poor imagery with irregular breathing.[12] Fantasies produced through relaxation may themselves deepen and intensify the state of relaxation, which in turn enlivens and extends the images. A reclining position tends to increase the flow of imagery—assuming, of course, that the person feels relaxed and comfortable in the setting. Because of the connotations of sex and subordination, many people are likely to be threatened if they are lying down in the presence of someone who is seated or standing. Once the fears are allayed, fantasy will flow more easily.[13] In one study, students were able to evoke earlier memories better when they were lying down than when they were seated.[14]

Sigmund Freud attributed the richness of dream imagery to the state of relaxation accompanying sleep. As the wardens of wakefulness go off duty, the phantasms emerge. Although letting go may usher in a state of intense reverie, however, it is not by itself sufficient for using images creatively. This is where a state of relaxed attention is necessary. It involves enough looseness to permit the images to emerge along with sufficient control to watch them and to occasionally direct their flow. If there is benefit to a skier or runner from imagining the next day's race, it is not in simple repetition but in improving performance through a better style or strategy until it becomes automatic and reflexive. I would not want to overdo the relaxation aspects of imagery except for enjoyment of one's inner life. Visualization training is not a lazy person's activity.

In Chapter 1, the possibility of using television as a means of improving imagery was mentioned. This seems a more logical medium for the task than print or radio. Many of the exercises that have been recommended for improving imagery would come across well on television. People can be more relaxed and languorous in their living rooms than in a theater or classroom, more able to attend to the interior camera and consider yesterday's dinner table, the voice of a wise grandmother, and the smells and feels of childhood. The pace of programing would have to be slowed down, periods of silence and a blank screen featured occasionally, and the announcer's voice kept soothing and encouraging. This is a radical departure from the frenetic keep-them-jumping stridency of commercial video. There would undoubtedly be irate calls to the station manager complaining about the lack of a picture on the screen. That is, in a sense, what imagery training is all about.

The goal of imagery training—and indeed of all education—should be the development of the capacity to switch back and forth between different modes of thinking as needed. This leaves open the question of when such switching is desirable. No one can answer this for all people in all circumstances. Society is benefited by the presence of people with a broad range of mental abilities. It is good to have some people who can consider issues without images and some who cannot lose their images no matter how hard they try. There is no sound basis for believing that pure abstraction is the highest form of reasoning. Loss of contact with the tangible world and detachment from experience are not virtues.

Vinous Memory

What visual imagery is to artists and architects, and auditory imagery is to composers and musicians, smell and taste imagery are to connoisseurs and professional food tasters. Through some combination of initial selection, formal training, and continued practice, people in these fields become expert in using a particular type of imagery. However, those who are proficient in one sensory modality tend also to be proficient in others. This is why terms such as *visile, audile, gustic,* or *motile* refer to relative strength rather than absolute levels of skill. The differences in thinking style between sensory and nonsensory thinkers are more apparent than those between people who rely on different senses. Most tasks involve several modalities simultaneously. An engineer concerned with bridges, roads, or traffic flow will probably need to emphasize visual and motor imagery; a textile designer will use both visual and tactile impressions; and the professional food taster will employ some combination of visual, tactile, olfactory, and gustatory responses.

By happy coincidence, I teach at a university with a renowned department of viticulture and enology, where students from all over the world, come to study the scientific aspects of grape-growing and wine-making. There is also a well-stocked wine cellar on campus, impressive testing and research laboratories, and one of the best wine libraries in the world. I am also very fond of good wine. All these seemed compelling arguments for investigating wnat was known about sensory memory in taste and smell. At the outset, I realized that the situations would not be identical to vision and hearing. Both smell and taste are evanescent. One quickly adapts to tastes and odors, but one can observe the statue of a discus thrower for hours, days, or weeks without its evocative powers being lessened. Its sensuality and kinetic potential are likely to *increase* as one carefully examines the arms and torso muscle by muscle. This is not the case with a finely prepared blue trout or a glass of fragrant chardonnay. The possibility of only fleeting impressions with taste and smell makes the topic of sensory memory tremendously important. Subsequent sips continue to have a pleasing taste, but the major portion of the enjoyment will be mnemonic—the capacity for later sips to evoke the images of the first delicate taste.

Discussing smell memory with enologists, I was struck with the parallels to visual imagery. Those who lack a memory for odors doubt that anyone has it, and those with a developed sensory memory think that everyone has the ability or the potential to develop a good nose. A nonimaging wine scientist told me flatly that a person might remember the idea of a smell, but not the smell itself. This was identical to what anoptic scientists have declared about pictures in the mind's eye.

Those rare individuals who can sometimes but not always identify type, region, vintner, and vintage from a single sip are similar in many ways to the eidetic imager or the composer with total aural recall. Wine expert H. W. Yoxall likens their talents to "the specialized skill of the person who regularly solves *The New York Times* crossword puzzle in less than half an hour. Such an individual has unusual mnemonic and associational powers, but is not necessarily more intelligent than the man without this particular gift."[15] Most wine experts believe that the ability to identify and appreciate wines can be learned. It is basically a matter of training and practice in using all the senses. The first thing a professional taster does is hold up the glass to light and examine it thoroughly, checking the color, the body, the presence of sediment or cork, and the characteristics of the liquid as it is swirled around in the bottom of the glass. The texture of the liquid is assayed by the touch receptors on the palate and the throat. Does the wine seem smooth? Rough? Velvety?

"Memory," wine-maker Louis Martini declared, "is a wine taster's greatest asset." [16] Wine connoisseur Michael Broadbent was described by his former employer in this way:

> With innate skill, intelligence, and hard work, he has reached his present eminent position in the wine circles and it is abundantly clear that he will continue to rise to greater heights. All these attributes are enhanced by a musical ear and considerable aptitude for drawing and painting. Undoubtedly it is precisely these talents which have aided his career in the art of wine. [17]

The rule in training wine tasters is the familiar formula of practice plus feedback:

> It is by frequent tasting, by making comparisons, by the examination of good types, that the delicacy and sensibility of the palate is developed, which enables it to detect and appreciate the faintest aroma, flavor, or bouquet, as well as the slightest defect. [18]

Robert Balzer's wine-tasting manual recommends blind tasting as a good training device. He does not mean visual blindfolding but, rather, intellectual blindfolding. The person tastes the wine while looking at it, but without seeing the label or knowing anything about it. Such information is, nonetheless, critical *after* the wine has been sipped. Without feedback as to the type, region, and vintage, the value of the experience as a training exercise is lost. There is nothing more frustrating for a wine connoisseur than to remember having tasted a wine before—but nothing else about it. It is no accident that most wine experts are extremely knowledgeable about the technical details of grape-growing and wine-making. Knowledge of grape-growing regions is essential. This is another curious connection between imagery and geography. The fleeting taste images must be tied to something substantial, and since bottles for particular kinds of wine tend to be uniform, the best available mnemonic is geographic.

There is an important difference between the sensory evaluation of wine and true tasting. The basis of most evaluation is reduction into constituent qualities. Science has reduced the basic odor qualities to *fragrant, fruity, putrid, spicy, burnt,* and *resinous.* While these terms are useful for filling out rating scales, they are not very helpful in describing the delicate bouquet or aroma of a fine wine. To convey the experience to others, something more is required, and this is simile, metaphor, and analogy. Beaujolais is compared to ripe strawberries; the aroma of burgundy to violets. Burgundy also feels velvety. This involves more than knowing the most luminous and tactile adjectives or catchy phrases. Without gustic and osmic imagery, the words are empty shells. The taste of wine can arouse images in all the modalities, from the climb up the hillside to examine the scraggly vines to the sound of the cask as it is tapped and of footsteps reverberating through the dark cellar sheltered from the summer heat.

Images do not always communicate well in words. The glass of wine that one person finds "austere, spartan, with a touch of boldness," another person describes as "quiet, honest, with a touch of class and finesse." Adrienne Lehrer found that people's descriptions of a wine were affected most by how much they liked it. Those who disliked a wine tended to call it sweet; those who liked it labeled it dry. In one experiment, people were paired up, and each person tasted three wines and wrote descriptions of them. Then each was asked to match up the partner's descriptions with the actual wines. People did little better than if they had flipped coins to make their decisions. In the hopes that more sophisticated judges might do better, she formed a panel of people who considered themselves to have especially sensitive palates. The panel met and each person sampled the wine in the presence of the group, and then they all discussed it and agreed upon a common description. Even this proved to have little communicative value. Other judges who tasted the wines were no more likely to choose the panel's

Sensory training (wine-tasting). Have a friend bring over a bottle of
wine with the label removed. Taste it. Try to identify the wine from its
aroma, bouquet, density, color, etc. Check your guess.

description than they were a fanciful description concocted by Lehrer. The judges matched wines they liked with the most favorable descriptions.

The unreliable and subjective nature of image language is one reason professional food tasters employ the basic taste qualities such as *sweet, sour, fruity, resinous,* and so on. Trained judges can estimate such qualities reliably. Vivid imagery is not essential in scientific wine tasting. It does, however, add much to the richness of experience. Adrienne Lehrer suggests that the metaphorical language of wine serves social purposes, too. Like discussions of drama, art, or music, the words indicate interest and permit people to share an experience even if each has experienced it differently.[19]

Identifying a wine can be a purely intellectual act. At a dance party, the host called over wine taster Robert Balzer and asked him to identify a half-filled glass. Balzer held the glass up to the brightest light available, swirled its bowl gently to agitate the pale gold liquid, sniffed it, sipped it, swallowed once, and returned the glass to his host. To everyone's amazement, he identified the brand and the vintage. Afterward, he described his method:

> By analysis, it was as much mental deduction as wine-tasting. The host, the late Harvey Mudd, was a distinguished wine lover and true connoisseur. He would certainly have selected champagne for the guests at his table. But the wine held out to me, while white, showed no trace of effervescence. When swirled in the glass, an almost imperceptible thread of fine bubbles told me it was in truth champagne, or at least a sparkling wine, and in the world of wine there are many of these but not many that a connoisseur would select for this occasion. It had to be one of the great names. Of those, in my experience, only Dom Perignon had such delicate carbonation as to lose its bubbly characteristics relatively quickly. The Ambassador Hotel (where the dance was held) was the only place I knew which still had any supply of that splendid, highly prized vintage of 1949. It had to be that one wine—and it was![20]

For wine appreciation, vividness of imagery would be more important than control. In general, control would not be necessary unless one worked for a vintner. Then it could be used to mentally blend different grapes until the right taste was achieved. This type of memory would require exercises to develop both liveliness and control.

Mescaline and LSD will improve vividness of imagination without, unfortunately, improving control. This is one reason why such drugs have been almost valueless in solving practical problems. In the research on psychedelic drugs, I am aware of only one controlled study showing a documented improvement in creativity.[21] Here, the drug session was preceded by relaxation exercises and discussions in which the participants were told that they would enjoy the drug session and find it productive. It is conceivable that training in the control of visualization would enable people to make more productive use of drug imagery and dream imagery.

Lacking a developed sense memory, one can only recall the categories of a memorable meal—the name of the restaurant, the menu, what one ate (beef wellington) and drank (thirty-year-old burgundy) and that the meal was worth remembering. Thus is a memorable meal classified and filed away in memory banks. The loss is in the replay. Accurate recall of the factual information will be no substitute for the picture of the steward decanting the liquid from the sediment and the candlelight glow; the trail of the red liquid as it is swirled around the bottom of the glass; the aroma, bouquet, fragrance almost filling the room; and of course its taste—like crushed raspberries, like wet leaves lying on the forest floor, or like a spring rain. To the person with a finely developed vinous memory, to be able to taste a wine without recalling it afterward would be a curse.

It is fairly easy to conceive of practice exercises in vinous mnemonics. One could extend the McKim and Hooper exercises into new modalities. The person might be encouraged to taste wines blindfolded; to photograph various wines to increase attentiveness to clarity, light, and visual effervescence; to compare drops of the wine as a painter might apply them to a fresh canvas; to taste a few drops on the tongue without swallowing them; to taste the same wine chilled and at room temperature; to experience the wine in fantasy and match this with the actual taste, and so on.

10
The Image Therapies

> The psychotherapist attempts to re-establish the original
> and normal imagery levels of consciousness in the patient
> by exposing him to critical areas of experience in a slow
> and systematic manner. . . . He takes each piece of criti-
> cal mental imagery experience and replays it to the patient
> repeatedly to disclose details.
>
> (AKHTER AHSEN)

Joseph Shorr, in his book *Psychotherapy Through Imagery,* maintains that virtually every major school of psychotherapy works with
the client's imagery to some degree.[1] Most methods borrow from
Freud and Jung the notion that images are the language of the unconscious. Whereas Freud considered it necessary to translate pictures into words so that the person could understand and deal with
them, the image therapies try to resolve problems on a fantasy
level, thus shortcutting the need for verbal translation. In the
beginnings of psychoanalysis, when Freud still used hypnosis, imagery was very important in treatment. Even after hypnosis was
rejected in favor of free association, many of the remnants of this
period remained—the couch, the attitude of relaxation, the patient
lying down. Patients were encouraged to close their eyes in order to
bring out more vivid images. Freud abandoned hypnosis first, then

physical touch, and finally patients were told to open their eyes as they talked. Psychoanalysis was to become more of a verbal than a visual technique, and the sessions more like conversations than dreaming.[2] Jerome Singer raises the question of whether Freud erred in not insisting on imagery alone rather than allowing patients to shift to verbal free associations. He might have thereby succeeded in penetrating the patient's unconscious more rapidly. We can only speculate how psychoanalysis might have evolved had its emphasis been on visual rather than verbal thinking. It might have attracted a different sort of person as therapist and appealed to a different sort of client. It might not be as intellectual and tedious a procedure as it is today.

Many types of therapy do not make a clear distinction between verbal and pictorial imagination. A patient is asked to imagine a situation that has some personal meaning and to describe it. Often it doesn't make much difference to the therapist whether the patient's fantasies are visual or not. Joseph Shorr asks his clients to picture situations as a means of provoking discussion and effect. Asking a client to mentally place a flower between his mother's breasts arouses more emotion and discussion than merely asking him how attracted he is to his mother. Shorr uses cathartic fantasies in which the person imagines traumatic experiences, task imagery such as escaping from an airplane wreck or building a bridge across a chasm, and tactile images of touching and being touched. These procedures tax the imagination of the therapist to project himself or herself into the patient's inner world. Commonly shared images between therapist and client will increase rapport. When the client asks, ''Do you remember the dream when I was alone in the forest?'' and the therapist can recall the scene in detail, it conveys more interest and feeling than when the therapist replies, ''No, tell me about it,'' or ''What do you think brought that into your mind?''[3] Anyone using these techniques must be aware of the wide variations in imagination. A visile therapist might interpret a verbal patient's lack of images as resistance, while a verbal therapist might be overwhelmed by the dramatic and vibrant inner camera of a sensory thinker. What would Freud have thought of superimager S., for whom numbers aroused tastes and odors as well as colors and

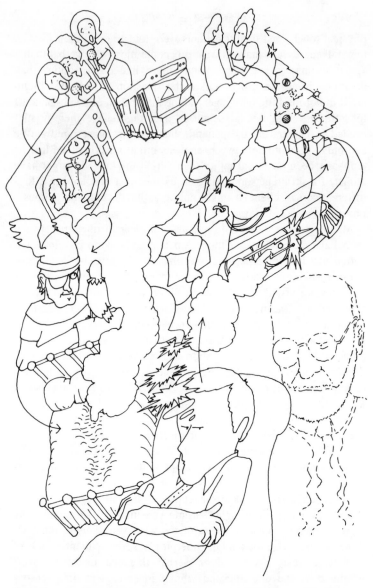

Had the superimager S. been Freud's patient, psychoanalysis might have taken a different course—more visual, less verbal.

sounds? Had S. found his way to Freud's office, psychoanalysis might have taken a different course.

Freud did not regard himself as a visual thinker. He stated that his earliest childhood memories were the only ones of a visual character that he ever experienced.[4] His other memories took the form of ideas rather than pictures. When Freud's associate Karl Abraham treated a patient with luminous recall of his infancy, Abraham interpreted this as suppressed voyeurism.[5] Analyst Bertram Lewin was surprised to find that many of his colleagues spontaneously generated images of their own in response to a patient's fantasies.[6]

Psychosynthesis is a therapy that relies heavily on symbolic visualization to bridge the gulf between the waking intellect and deeper layers of personality. The therapist uses spontaneous daydreams and sleep dreams to identify specific problems, and then controlled visualization to direct messages back into the unconscious. It is assumed that the unconscious will be more responsive to communications coming in its own language: images. Robert Gerard, a practitioner of this technique, asks his clients to imagine specific objects, and then, based on what they visualize, he follows this up with training sessions to resolve problems. When asked to visualize a rose, a repressed patient could picture only a rosebud unable to open. Gerard then embarked on imagery training in which the patient, over a period of time, learned to visualize the bud originally shut tight and then gradually opening up and growing into a beautiful rose. The effectiveness of the technique, according to Gerard, depends upon the connection between the symbol itself, in this case a rose, and deeper layers of the personality. Symbols are selected for their therapeutic value for the patient. A person having difficulty getting along with others might be asked to visualize two hands clasping each other. If one of the hands is wet and clammy, the patient works at this mentally until the problem is resolved and a firm, dry, tension-free grasp is made. A woman who desires to reconstruct her personality might be asked to visualize the creation of a garden step by step. Every day she imagines a little more of an empty field being transformed through intensive cultivation into a beauty spot.[7]

Spontaneous reveries are used by therapists to identify problem areas. The therapist plays an active role in guiding the fantasies. The client who imagines a frightening lion pursuing him may be asked to make friends with the lion. This could require several sessions. Guided daydreams differ from ordinary reveries in that the person is encouraged to deal actively with the problem rather than running away to another dream. Cues or visual aids are sometimes used to direct a patient's attention to particular topics. A photograph placed on a nearby table or a white card with the word *happiness* printed on it will affect the direction of the patient's fantasies. Roberto Assagioli uses evocative words printed in complementary colors to induce specific moods; for example, *calm* printed in dark green letters, *courage* in red letters, *serenity* in deep blue. He believes that visual images suggested by these words will intersect with the client's unconscious.[8]

Other therapists use music to arouse and guide imagery. The selections played are chosen for their specific therapeutic value. A patient who has difficulty expressing aggressive feelings may be asked to conjure up images while listening to the "1812 Overture," and someone who seems driven and unable to relax may be asked to picture scenes while listening to Beethoven's Sixth Symphony ("Pastorale").

Another therapist who takes fantasy seriously, Wilson Van Dusen, gives these rules for using it therapeutically:

1. The inner life comes out more easily when the person is relaxed.
2. With practice, visualization can be greatly intensified until a person can see colored scenes at any time.
3. To learn from the process, one must feel into the dramatic language of the inner life in order to read back how it reflects one's self.
4. The process can be used to learn what one's body has to say, to clarify impressions of another person, to portray a mood so as to better understand its methods, and to project one's inner values to better understand one's natural inclinations.

Van Dusen takes subjective experience so seriously that he has, upon occasion, conversed with characters in his patients' dreams as well as with people in the hallucinations of hospitalized schizophrenics. Learning to talk with the voices helped him establish contact with the patient. He soon found that the voices were afraid of him, since they did not want to be analyzed and discarded. Van Dusen believes that hallucinations are the eruptions into consciousness of what is ordinarily unconscious. Treatment involves either getting the patient to reduce an abnormal dependence upon inner creations or to somehow unite with them in a higher order of consciousness.

Van Dusen is less active than most other therapists in proposing images. He relies heavily on the spontaneous fantasy life that emerges when the person is relaxed. He regards the translation of feelings into images as a positive sign, since it gives the client and the therapist more access to them. Visualization training used with this method involves spontaneous rather than controlled imagery. It is based on becoming sufficiently relaxed to let the images emerge and then exercising greater sensitivity in attending to them. This in itself, Van Dusen believes, increases the clarity and the frequency of images.[9]

Desensitization training would seem to be the opposite of sensitivity training, but it isn't. It is rather a guided journey into fear in order to overcome it. Some fears, of course, are justified, but others are not. Desensitization therapy, as practiced by Joseph Wolpe, confronts the individual with small doses of anxiety in a nonthreatening situation.[10] The rationale is that every time a person confronts his specter without frightening consequences, his trepidation will diminish. Therapy begins with the person writing down an anxiety hierarchy. This is a list of fright-related situations, from most feared to least feared. The person afraid of snakes might consider handling a live snake to be at the top of his list (most feared) and looking at a card with the word *snake* at the bottom of the list, with perhaps a line drawing of a snake one step up, a photograph of a snake two steps up, and so on.

Following the construction of the list, the therapist gives the client relaxation training, such as breathing exercises, body work, or meditation. Therapy begins with the least-feared situations on the client's list, such as looking at the word *snake*. As he holds the card in his hand, the client engages in breathing exercises until he feels completely relaxed. Obviously the card itself is not going to bite him. Once he can hold the card and say that he feels perfectly calm, the therapist moves on to the next situation, which might be a drawing of a snake. At some point, the therapist will use fantasy equivalents instead of pictures. The client is asked to imagine himself walking on a path and seeing a snake fifteen feet away or visiting the reptile area of the zoo and watching a caged snake. Fantasy experiences are important, since many frightening situations cannot be brought into the therapist's office. People whose fears of snakes were desensitized were able to stand closer to a live snake in a controlled experiment than people who had spent the same amount of time talking about their fears or listening to lectures about snakes. The same approach, although lacking a fancy name, is frequently used to desensitize stage fright or fear of public speaking.

When someone who is a good imager is unable to visualize something, the object or person probably has some emotional significance. Political cartoonists, who are usually considered excellent imagers, often have difficulty visualizing people they find particularly loathsome. During World War II, some cartoonists could draw Hitler only by making him ridiculous and thus omitting the murderous qualities of the man's character. Cartoonist Jules Feiffer disliked former President Nixon so intensely that he was unable to visualize him, and therefore could not draw Nixon properly.[11]

Therapists have learned that pleasant images can be used to reward certain behaviors and unpleasant images to discourage behaviors. Covert positive reinforcement is the technique used by therapist Joseph Cautela to encourage clients. First he discovers scenes or places that bring delight or pleasure to the client. A client might have very strong ties to the coast and enjoy imagining the cool surf rolling in over the sands, the salt spray in the air, the waves breaking at a distance, the feeling of himself surfing, swimming, or just lying on the beach. This fantasy is used as a reward for thoughts that the therapist wants to encourage. For a client who had difficulty expressing himself to women, the therapist would instruct him to imagine himself talking to a woman; as soon as the image is clear, the client switches to thoughts of the seashore. This sequence is repeated in a variety of social situations. Every time the client is able to get a clear image of himself talking to a woman without embarrassment, he can reward himself by imagining his favorite beach. Cautela cites numerous studies indicating that covert positive reinforcement is successful in encouraging people to overcome fears.[12]

The same method, but with unpleasant images, can be used to discourage patterns of behavior. If a client is afraid of creepy, crawly creatures, this image can be used to get his mind back to his immediate problem, say a fear of elevators. The therapist instructs him first to think about rats, mice, and other vermin crawling around his arm, but then to terminate that image by seeing himself entering an elevator, calm and confident. The elevator becomes a safe haven every time rodents are imagined. When the therapist says "switch," the client is to immediately terminate the unpleasant image and focus on a positive scene, that is, entering an elevator and feeling good about it.[13]

Another approach is to associate an undesirable behavior with a horrible image. The alcoholic could be asked to imagine vomit all over the liquor bottle and a poisonous spider inside the bottle. Some studies report this technique effective in helping people become less tense, lose weight, and control their drinking, while other studies do not support this.[14] There is no guarantee in this approach, of course, that the client who says he is imagining a terrible scene at the therapist's behest is actually doing so. It seems likely that clients would not have the same reluctance to imagine pleasant scenes.

Covert extinction is a technique used to deny a client the usual rewards obtained from engaging in undesirable behaviors. The client who wants to lose weight will be asked to imagine eating but to feel nothing—no taste, no smell, no sensations of any kind; just a deadness. Because it avoids the unpleasantness of imagining horrible scenes, there are fewer ethical problems involved in using the method, and clients might be more willing to imagine these kinds of nonfeeling scenes.[15]

Clients may also be asked to imagine other people doing things that they are afraid to do. The principle here is one of using the behavior of others as a model. Imaginary modeling has been found to be especially useful in encouraging assertive behavior. Individuals who were able to imagine people resembling themselves being outspoken have been able to increase their own assertiveness.[16]

Thus, imagery can be used not only to encourage people to explore unknown territories and confront their devils, but to reward certain patterns of behavior by linking them to pleasant images and to discourage other activities by linking them to unpleasant thoughts. This represents an extension of learning theory into the realm of fantasy. At the moment, it requires a near leap of faith to believe that changing fantasy will eventually change behavior, but as experiments demonstrating the effectiveness of the approach begin to accumulate, the case grows stronger. Thus far, the available evidence indicates that the use of desirable and satisfying images is more effective than techniques involving harsh and punitive imagery.

The Exorcists

Just as relaxation facilitates imagery, the reverse is also true. Many of the current body-work techniques extend their impact through imagery. Moshe Feldenkrais, whose exercises have benefited numerous people with physical disabilities, follows many of his procedures with a fantasy replay. After the person has done a complicated kneeling-bending procedure twenty-five times, he is encouraged to lie down on his stomach and mentally repeat all the different movements his body has gone through. He is asked to imagine the motor sensations in his muscles and bones, going so far as to tense his muscles slightly but without discernible movement. The mental exercise is not a substitute for the physical activity but an extension of it that gives the person more contact with and control over muscles and limbs.[17]

Richard Suinn, an advisor to several Olympic teams, uses visual-motor rehearsal to reduce tensions that interfere with athletic performance. His technique involves three stages—relaxation, visualization training, and the use of imagery to improve motor skills. Because of the nature of athletic performance, there is a heavy emphasis on tactile and motor imagery. Suinn first tested out his approach on the University of Colorado ski team. Attempting to do a controlled experiment, he worked with only half the team, who mentally rehearsed their races. The procedure worked so well that the experiment was never completed: The ski coach was so impressed by the performance of the imagery group that he selected only its members for the competition, and thus no comparison between them and the control group was possible. It is perhaps relevant that the chosen team went on to win several trophies. This kind of "inner game" differs significantly from the post mortem required by many coaches using videotapes. These review sessions tend to be retrospective and to emphasize errors. Visual-motor rehearsal requires people to mentally overcome their mistakes, thus preparing them to do better next time.[18]

Techniques that require a person to confront images and deal with them directly require a higher level of visualization than approaches that use imagery primarily as a diagnostic tool. The athlete or neurotic patient who "cannot imagine" a situation isn't going to get much benefit from a fantasized encounter. Except for psychosynthesis and Suinn's mental rehearsal, most therapies do not include specific training in visualization.

Jerome Singer found that overweight college students did not differ from thin students in the amount of time they spent daydreaming, but that they did have less visual imagery. When they tried to summon up fantasies, the fat students shut their eyes, as if desperately trying to shut out the external stimulation. The poverty of inner mental life and dependence upon external stimulation was seen by Singer as contributing to the excessive responsiveness of the fat person to food placed in front of him or her. Giving such people greater control of their imagery through visualization training may be a means of reducing their excessive dependence upon external stimulation.[19]

The imagery therapies strive to remedy the detachment that many people feel from themselves—not only from their bodies, but from their minds as well. To understand this seeming contradiction, we must recognize the distinction between the *I* and the *me,* the *knower* and the *known.* I am the knower of my life, my past is what is known. Reducing the stuff of experience to a computer printout detaches me from my past. The image therapies, in retaining and developing the pictorial qualities of one's recollections, reverse the trend toward abstraction and prevent too wide a schism between the I and the me. Things remain stored in consciousness in much the same form that they came in, retaining their smoothness, color, softness, and heaviness. For the sensory thinker, the world of the mind bears a direct physical resemblance to the world outside.

In his book *Psycho-imagination Therapy,* Joseph Shorr remarks, "At the beginning of therapy some individuals may feel that they do not possess a vivid or intense imagination. . . . Consequently, they may be amazed to discover that with proper guidance and encouragement, their imaginations flow easily."[20] Shorr seems to assume either that this capacity exists in everyone and will develop automatically through practice, or that his anoptic clients will of their own accord terminate a procedure that is frustrating and unproductive for them. The verbal-minded no doubt will be more comfortable in encounter groups, client-centered therapy, or some other approach that puts more emphasis on words than images. But though the abstract thinker will find a word-dominated therapy more congenial, the solution to his detachment from experience probably lies in less talk and more feeling. People who want to change their mental or emotional patterns may be advised to deliberately seek out methods that encourage new styles of thinking. For the abstract, word-dependent individual, this can mean image therapy; for the concrete person driven by feeling, a more intellectual approach such as existential analysis may be preferable.

It would be undesirable to match therapists and patients according to their thinking styles in any absolute sense. The analogy to a marriage is apt. Sometimes a marriage works when the partners are very much alike and can share common interests, but a marriage may be equally successful between two people whose divergent interests make them complementary to one another. I would *not* automatically recommend that a visual-minded patient consult a visual-minded therapist or a verbal-minded patient consult a verbal-minded therapist. There would be numerous instances and often compelling reasons for a person seeking change to select a therapist who had a different style of thinking. No one wants to pay fifty dollars an hour to look into a mirror. What is necessary is that whichever therapist the patient selects, each should have an understanding of and respect for how the other thinks.

11

Mental Maps

Eskimos live at the Arctic margin of the inhabited world. They did not, however, know this until they came into contact with large numbers of white men. Before the encounter they saw their habitat not only as the world's geographical center but also as its cultural and population center.

(Yi-Fu Tuan)

I have never visited Moscow, but I have a mental representation that includes everything I have read, heard, and seen of it. This picture includes the long lines of people in drab clothing waiting to enter Lenin's Tomb, the spaciousness of the mosaic-decorated subway stations, the Kremlin and the Moscow University skyscraper, the spires of orthodox churches around the city, the lack of cars (and litter) on the streets, the crowded department stores, female construction workers, the harsh winter, and so on. Lacking any direct experience with Moscow, these scenes as I imagine them have very little spatial character. I do not know where the Kremlin is with reference to Moscow University or Lenin's Tomb, although I assume they all lie "downtown." For them to become spatial would require movement through the area or else a city map, and I am not likely to consult a map of Moscow unless I am actually going to visit it.

Mental maps are the meeting place of geography and psychology. Because they include odors, sounds, and sociopolitical information, they are richer and more varied than cartographers' maps. To the extent that they distort and omit significant items, they are more variable and biased. My image of San Francisco, a city I have visited many times, is a hodgepodge of neighborhoods, landmarks, freeways, familiar streets, friends' houses, restaurants, factories, and business offices. The spatial attributes are spotty, selective, and personal. Cartographic maps are necessary for traveling on land or sea, but they are much less useful in predicting where people will want to go and what they will want to do when they get there.

Our images of places are highly personal. Places that are important to us tend to be more vivid, detailed, and exaggerated in scale. Maps drawn by students in Finland, Canada, Sierra Leone, and the United States showed that people enlarged the size of familiar areas and reduced the size of unfamiliar places. Within a single country, nearby places were remembered best and were the most detailed. In addition, large areas tend to be better remembered than small areas; for example, the exaggerated importance given to Texas and Alaska in the United States. However, when a place is outstandingly small, such as Rhode Island or Luxembourg, it can become distinctive on that basis. Boundary locations are prominent in mental maps because they mark off one area from another. Borders acquire strategic importance in frontier disputes, customs inspections, immigration processing, and so on.[1] Cultural factors, such as the antipathy between English- and French-Canadians, will affect the content of regional imagery. Quebec residents, living in the heart of French Canada, tend to have Quebec-centered mental maps. Most long-distance calls from Montreal go to other French-speaking cities in Quebec. Matching for size and distance and adjusting for cost, a call from Quebec is five times more likely to be destined for another Quebec city than to a city in the adjacent province of Ontario.[2]

Terrence Lee was curious about why people patronized a shopping center in their own city when the shopping center of a nearby town was geographically closer. Examining the mental maps of the residents, he found that people consistently overestimated the distances to out-of-town stores and facilities.[3] Testing Lee's belief that satisfaction with the city center led to a shortening of perceived distance toward the downtown area, Robert Potter surveyed consumers in Stockport, England, where approximately the same number of shopping centers were located uptown and downtown. He found that twice as many people shopped in a downtown direction and that people possessed more accurate information about stores in the central business district.[4]

Distance is more than a matter of kilometers; it includes time and cost as well. When college students from Columbus, Ohio, were asked to estimate the distance from their homes to other parts of the city, downtown places were judged to be further away than uptown places, even when the distances were equivalent. This distortion was attributed to the multiplicity of barriers, the density of buildings and traffic downtown, and the variations in color, height, function, and activity as well as the greater time required to travel downtown.[5]

People who live downtown tend to overestimate the distance to outlying areas and to underestimate the distances from outlying areas into the central city. A colleague teaching at Clark University describes this as the Worcester Effect. His friends in Boston were continually inviting him in from Worcester for meetings, social gatherings, or to speak to their students. He usually accepted these invitations, since he enjoyed the cultural amenities of Boston and had many friends there. Yet he learned that whenever he invited Boston people to Worcester, they always found excuses not to come: the trip was too long, there was snow or rain or fog, the trip was dull, there was nothing to see along the way.

My wife and I escape to the California coast on occasional weekends. Two of the more desirable destinations in terms of scenery, restaurants, and shopping are Monterey and Mendocino. There is a curious discrepancy in distance between our mental maps and the actual distances. Mendocino seems much closer than Monterey because the road runs entirely through rural and semirural terrain. On some stretches of the two-lane road, one will not see another car for fifteen minutes. The trip to Monterey is all freeway and mostly urban. One must be constantly alert for other drivers who travel at the speed limit and beyond. The trip is nerve-racking and tiresome. We don't go to Monterey very often, because it doesn't seem in our orbit. On the map, however, Monterey is at least seventy-five miles closer and an hour's less driving time, but psychologically it is further away than Mendocino. Judgments of far and near are, within considerable limits, more psychological than actual. To the child who has lived all his life in Harlem, the downtown area of Manhattan will seem inordinately far and the Palisades of New Jersey across the river to be in another country. Almost everyone can find similar discrepancies in distance between their mental maps and AAA maps. It may occur with regard to a favorite shopping center—the downtown bias mentioned earlier—or a favorite skiing resort or a theater or lake. Those places that are closer to us psychologically appear closer in distance, even though at some level we recognize that they are not.

A return journey usually seems shorter than the trip to a place, and large geographic units tend to swallow up smaller ones. Most people imagine that San Diego is southwest of Reno. Actually, it is southeast. Because California is west of Nevada, we therefore assume that San Diego must be west of Reno. We also know that Canada is north of the United States. However, if you make this assumption in Detroit, you will see the sun rising in the west and setting in the east. People in Eugene, Oregon, who think of Highway 99 as a north-south axis will occasionally see the sun rising in the north. The explanation is that Highway 99 bends as it passes through Eugene. People can give more rapid estimates about the direction one state lies from another (Michigan–Utah) than between cities (Detroit–Salt Lake City). The greater time lag with cities occurs when people transform cities into higher order units (states) before making their judgments.[6]

Mental maps contain *location data* and *attributive data*. Location includes distance and direction, which can be measured in either travel time, effort, or money. I have only a vague idea of the geographic location of Kenya and whether it would be quicker to fly west or east to get there, yet a call to the travel agent will tell me how much the trip will cost and how long it will take, the two elements with most direct relevance to me. Attributive data contain descriptive and evaluative elements. Descriptive elements include the structural and physical characteristics of the environment—the height of the buildings, the width of streets, the colors of signs and billboards. Evaluational elements include the more subjective aspects, for example, whether we think a building is modern or old-fashioned, attractive or ugly, elegant or gaudy.

The human perceptual apparatus has evolved to take advantage of experience while the body is in motion. We localize sounds most accurately when we can move our heads, and we can determine the shape of objects accurately as we explore them with our hands. The information produced by our movement through space is essential for our cognitive maps of the environment.[7] Movement also aids in the development of perceptual constancy, which is the ability to recognize objects independent of the angle of view, distance, or light conditions. Five-year-old children in Massachusetts and in small villages in Puerto Rico could accurately interpret maplike representations and aerial photographs of villages and showed extreme pleasure in doing so. Children could arrange toy houses, toy cars, and toy trains, and place them at a reasonable scale on a maplike area containing roads, hills, simulated water, and other geographic features. Children who had never seen the earth from a vertical perspective could both recognize and arrange objects on it sensibly. Since the children had never interacted with such large spaces, one could only assume the existence of highly developed cognitive maps in these five-year-olds.[8]

According to Jean Piaget, a child's first conception in space is egocentric. All directions and objects are oriented in respect to her body. When asked by Piaget to describe the location of something in her house, the child replies, "It's over there," or "It's over this way," indicating the location with respect to self. Only later does the child take an objective frame of reference and locate objects with respect to fixed landmarks such as doors, windows, mommy's room, and so on. Eventually the child progresses to a fully abstract reference scheme using compass points or, in other cultures, the sun, the stars, or places of religious significance.[9]

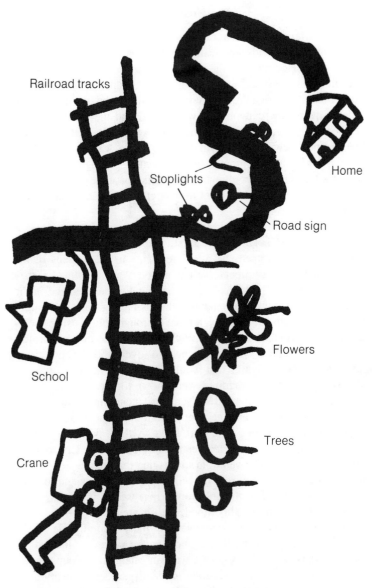

Railroad tracks

Stoplights

Road sign

Home

Flowers

School

Trees

Crane

A five-year-old's map of the bus trip between home and school, a distance of about three miles.

Cities differ in their imageability based on the distinctiveness of buildings, actual landscape features, and local culture.[10] Psychologist Kristina Hooper uses the term *superfeatures* for those distinctive elements that set one area or building apart from others.[11] Manhattan's superfeatures include its skyline, the neon circus at Times Square, the canyons of Wall Street, and the winding mews of Greenwich Village. Superfeatures are so important that the outline of one, New York's skyline, for example, can be recognized more quickly and accurately than an actual photograph. Hooper suggests that city maps showing landmarks or important buildings out of scale will be more helpful in orienting a tourist than a true scale map.

Stanley Milgram has investigated New Yorkers' awareness of city districts and landmarks.[12] First, employing a technique used earlier by Kevin Lynch, he asked residents to draw maps of the city, listing all the streets, neighborhoods, and landmarks they could think of.[13] The typical map was found to be localized in the downtown area, with many neighborhoods having no tangible representation. He then undertook a more thorough study, using photographs from random settings throughout the entire city. A professional photographer was dispatched to over 150 locations and instructed to take pictures that would convey the most information to a viewer. These photographs were shown to two hundred people recruited from newspaper advertisements, including residents from all neighborhoods in all age groups, although most were young adults in their twenties who had lived in their particular neighborhoods between five and ten years and in New York City most of their lives. The people were told to imagine that they were viewing the slides as passengers from the window of a tour bus and to write in an answer booklet the location of the scene in terms of its borough, its specific neighborhood, and its street.

Not surprisingly, Manhattan was the most recognizable of the five boroughs. Almost all the photographs correctly located by three-quarters of the respondents were in Manhattan. People in all boroughs were also more accurate in identifying street locations in Manhattan than anywhere else. A resident of Brooklyn, for example, was more likely to correctly identify a Manhattan scene than one in his own borough. The nondescript quality of Queens was apparent in the errors made. When a person didn't know the location of a scene, he tended to place it in Queens.

Mental maps reveal differential travel patterns and experiences within an area. The mental map of a Grosse Point commuter will be full of detail about his suburb and the downtown business district but impoverished regarding the adjacent residential areas. A young black child growing up in Detroit is likely to draw a map rich in detail of his or her own neighborhood and to omit the suburbs.

Specialized Maps

Because mental maps include more than geographic information, they have many specialized uses. When youngsters in Philadelphia were asked to indicate dangerous places in the city, their drawings showed the danger spots centering around the headquarters and turf of street gangs.[14] Mental maps can also be used to identify desirable locations. Pacific Coast states which are looked upon as attractive living and working places have experienced population growth. The Great Plains states, identified in mental maps as less desirable, have been an area of marked migrational loss.[15] Research on the mental maps of schoolchildren is currently underway in England; authorities hope this will enable them to predict future migration trends. In prison, inmates and staff will have similar (and generally accurate) maps of the relative desirability of various tiers and buildings. This is also true of mental institutions. Branch offices of corporations and government agencies will be known by employees as more or less desirable locations. In FBI circles, it was understood that transfer to the Butte, Montana, office meant that the person had fallen into disfavor at headquarters. Certain district offices of large corporations are regarded as springboards to success, while others are backwashes. A commercial traveler has an internal map featuring good sales areas, motels, and restaurants. Burglars identify areas of opportunity with the fuzzy borders between distinct

residential neighborhoods. These transition zones provide an anonymity favorable to the burglar's operations, in contrast to neighborhood interiors, where strangers can be quickly identified.[16]

Although mental maps are multisensory, a person can construct a
map in a single modality if instructed to do so. Most investigators
have asked people to draw visual representations of cities—how
things look in terms of size, shape, color, and location. Russian
psychologist F. N. Shemyakin studied the mental maps of blind
children. Children who are blind from birth are still able to locate
objects and rooms in their own homes. In comparison with sighted
children, the details most likely to be omitted are the windows,
which have less significance for blind children.[17] They will still
enjoy being in rooms with windows that open, because windows
bring in outside sounds, thus enlarging their world from the tight
visual space of the room to the expansive auditory space of the city.
Windows have somewhat the same function for the blind as for the
sighted in transmitting information from the outside into enclosed
space.[18] On the basis of auditory, tactile, and motor cues, blind
people develop layouts of neighborhoods and cities with a reasonable degree of accuracy. Locations on their maps are marked by
sonic cues that are dependable and distinctive. These must be selected with care, because the sonic environment changes with
weather and time of day. A heavy rain or layer of snow can completely change the sonic environment of a place. Finding cues to
identify places in a city is not often a problem for the sighted person, who can rely upon road signs, street names, store names, and
other visual cues.

Smell Maps

The dependence upon vision of most sighted individuals obscures
experience in other modalities. Instructions to attend to a nonvisual
modality will result in a sensitivity to nuance never before experienced. I asked several students to construct smell maps of the
seventy-five-mile journey between Sacramento and San Francisco.
Their first response was incredulity and frustration. They protested
that they didn't know any odors, or maybe only one or two, and it

would be too difficult to describe them. Like most Americans, they lacked a descriptive vocabulary of smell. Even the word *smell* has negative connotations. It is complimentary to say that someone has taste or vision, but if you say he smells, watch out. He could conceivably smell good, but that isn't how the phrase would be taken. Many of the odors we try to hide are the natural and normal results of perfectly ordinary cooking, cleaning, and toilet activities. In the process of this suppression, we have become a nation of olfactory illiterates. This is unfortunate, as the human sense of odor is extraordinarily sensitive. It provides a rare instance in which the human is more perceptive than any machine. A person can detect minute quantities of materials in the air at levels that machines will register nothing. The extraordinary ability is generally wasted. Asking people to pay attention to their olfactory experiences is a step toward reversing the trend.

The smell map of the highway between Sacramento and San Francisco differs significantly from the visual map. Fragrances change with time and season because so many are agricultural and industrial. To experience them and know their significance is to be in tune with the rhythms and flux of valley life. Leaving Sacramento, depending upon wind direction, one savors a trace of the family barbecue emanating from the Presto Log factory southwest of the bridge. This merges with the pine odor of huge piles of wood chips waiting to be loaded for Japan. Sacramentans often also identify this area with the haze that drifts over the city in the spring and summer, the result of grain stubble ignited to hasten the planting of a second crop. Further on, there is the aroma of ketchup from the cannery. Some residents claim they can tell the flavor of ketchup being manufactured from the scent—pizza, mushroom, barbecue, or regular. By late August, the redolence of ketchup is overshadowed by the acrid smell of tomatoes rotting in the fields. The next city brings the sweet, musty smell of drying hay and, on its outskirts, a ranch growing aromatic herbs for the Spice Islands Company. (Only occasionally does any of the fragrance of this unusual farming operation reach the speeding driver.) A few miles further on, one encounters the bane of Vacaville residents—the aroma of dehydrated onions.

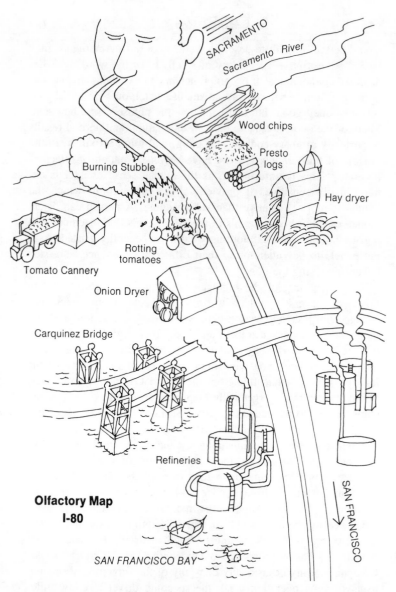

An olfactory map of Interstate 80 between Sacramento and San Francisco.

The next few cities don't have much in the way of a distinctive fragrance, at least along the freeway. One gets a slight whiff of salt air while crossing the Carquinez Straits, but this is quickly over-shadowed by the sharp odors from the Richmond refinery. The oil smell disappears as one approaches Berkeley, and the salt air re-places the valley heat remaining in the car. On still days in the summer, when the natural air-conditioning system of the region is out of service, smog hangs over the East Bay to offend eye and nostril. However, as one crosses the Bay Bridge, the salt air invigo-rates even the most jaded palate.

I do not suggest that all these odors are pleasant or interesting, any more than I feel that all the sights and sounds along the high-way are pleasant or interesting. Rather, they are all aspects of a de-veloping sensory panorama open to anyone who will experience it. Nor would I recommend that drivers sniff their way to San Fran-cisco along this busy stretch of road—the results might conceivably be lethal, since most of what one would inhale would be au-tomobile exhaust. The only safe way to experience the sensory qualities of this journey is to avoid the freeway wherever possible and take side roads. Whether one is walking, bicycling, or driving slowly with the windows open, one can enjoy the sounds, sights, and odors and inhale without fear of asphyxiation. A smell map along the side roads is incredibly richer and more detailed than on the freeway itself.

A kinesthetic (movement) map of the same journey would be even less detailed, because the road is well graded, with few no-ticeable curves. The three bridges would be major landmarks, since they involve changes in driving speed (two are toll bridges) and there would be vibrations both from the bridge and the wind. Other events would be the two mountain passes, which many drivers use to divide the journey into thirds. A flat, well-graded, and well-sur-faced freeway is not the ideal surface for constructing a movement map. Covering the same terrain on bicycle or on foot will result in a keener appreciation of grades, curves, textures, and the like.

A sound map of a freeway is similarly uninteresting. The road surface varies little except across the bridges, and the wind hitting the car would obscure all other noise except the occasional airplane overhead and vibrations from trucks and cars roaring by.

The sound maps of Mexican students showed the importance of time of day. Early morning was characterized by church bells, small birds, roosters, and cars. By noon, the strongest auditory elements were, in order: cars, bells, music, and airplanes. At night, the sounds were of serenades, music, cars, and once again, roosters. Even when a sound was reported throughout the entire day, there were still peak periods. Automobiles were heard throughout the entire day but were dominant at noon and afternoon. There was also a diurnal variation in these students' smell maps. Morning generally smelled good, fresh, and of flowers. Noon smelled of exhaust fumes and food preparation, although savoring the aroma of cooking food probably more than offset the unpleasantness of the automobile smells for many residents.[19]

Map or Metaphor?

Some geographers object to the term *map* being applied to such spotty and selective representations and consider this usage of *map* to be more metaphoric than anything else. A major anthology on the topic defines *mental maps* as "complex, highly selective, abstract, generalized representations in various forms."[20] The debate about whether geographical features as presented in mental maps are mainly visual or verbal has a familiar ring to it. The underlying issue is the role of sensory content in thinking. Geographer Yi-Fu Tuan regards imagery as a luxury in thinking, something akin to illustrations in a book or slides in a lecture—desirable but not necessary. Its value, he believes, is not apparent even for orientation. The person who is lost, he feels, needs a real map and not a subjective one—"recalling odd images of shop windows, street corners, and statues is of no help."[21] For orientation and navigation, Tuan maintains, one needs abstract schemata rather than mental pictures. This is the geographer's version of the behaviorist's criticism that imagery is a linguistic fiction. That is, they believe that people don't really think in pictures, they just describe their thinking this way because it makes sense to others.[22] In rebuttal, one can add that *mind* is a metaphor, *emotion* is a metaphor, *prejudice* is a metaphor, and so is anything intangible that we try to describe in words. If all mental phenomena are metaphorical (literally, a transfer from one realm to another), then the term itself does not add very much. One could also say that the names of all mental phenomena are words, but this too adds little. One should not confuse a word with a tangible object or the name of a psychological process with the process itself. *Mental imagery* is the name that people give to the pictures in their heads and the songs in their minds. It is obvious that these are not identical with photographs, moving pictures, or phonograph records. They are "something less" in that they contain fewer details and are less accurate, but to the extent that they are multisensory and controllable and permit invention and creative problem solving, they are "something more." A photograph is also a metaphor. This is obvious with a black-and-white print, but it is also true with color reproductions, which compress three dimensions into two and distort colors. Let us forget the pseudoissue that imagery is a metaphor; any psychological process is metaphorical in the same sense. The mental map, as a composite of all the sensory and verbal information that a person has about a place, is metaphorical, but it is also of practical value in orientation and in understanding the environmental choices people make.

As with other types of images, there is a persistent belief that mental maps are interesting but not very important. What "really counts" are the hard economic and demographic statistics. Images, if they have any reality at all, are ephemeral and trivial and can safely be ignored by policymakers. This position may be theoretically defensible but not practically so. I have never worked on a design project in which images were not important. Included here would be the employees' picture of their employer, the tenants' image of management in a housing project, or the local citizens' conception of city government. When we attempted to institute bicycle paths in the late 1960s, we encountered serious image problems. City officials considered the bicycle to be a child's toy or a recreational vehicle rather than a mode of transportation. When we requested room on the road for bike lanes, city officials who imagined bicycles as toys had an incongruous vision of cars speeding by a special lane reserved for children on tricycles. To change their minds (and policies), it was necessary to show photographs of adults bicycling to work or to school. We also had to overcome the hero image championed by touring and racing cyclists. Such hardy folk were so attuned to surviving in dangerous traffic that they couldn't understand why a cyclist would want reserved space. A bicycle lane seemed, to them, positively demeaning. It was necessary to convince them that less experienced cyclists had different needs which required different solutions. The touring cyclist wanted to get away from the city, but the transportation cyclist wanted to go downtown, and the needs of the racing cyclist were special. Once we understood these different images, we were in a better position to find suitable facilities for each group of riders.

12

The Colored Compass

> It is an elementary biological necessity for human beings to absorb color, to extract color. We must assume that there are conditions of color relationships and tensions, light values, forms, positions, directions which are common to all humans and determined by our physiological mechanisms.
>
> (LASZLO MOHOLY-NAGY)

Most information comes to us through our eyes, but this is supplemented by what we hear, smell, taste, and feel. These sense impressions are mixed together in very complex ways. They are not simply sight-plus-sound-plus-smell, but rather a network of associations, expectations, and sensory crossovers. For some people, sounds produce the experience of colors and odors awaken tactile impressions. These may be almost equal in intensity and quality to the actual experience, or they can be conceptual similarities between, for example, particular tones and geometric figures. Cross-modality transfers that contain distinct sensory elements are called *synesthesias*. The mnemonist S. discussed in Chapter 6 had vivid synesthesias. The two most common synesthesias are colored hearing and colored taste. Famed psychologist E. B. Titchener, an eidetiker who experienced frequent synesthesias, declared, "I never

sit down to read a book or to write a paragraph, or to think out a
problem, without a musical accompaniment. Usually the accompaniment is orchestral, with a predominance of woodwind."[1] Such
people have no need for the piano that would play colors and the
organ that would display light that engaged Sir Isaac Newton and
so many other scientists, composers, and artists after him.
Titchener is known today for his advocacy of introspection, or the
analysis of sensory experience in terms of elements or basic mental
intent. It seems no accident that an eidetic imager would take mental life seriously. Paradoxically, Titchener's extremely high standards for describing the qualities of inner life were partly responsible for the demise of introspection as a research tool in psychology.
People lacking Titchener's great powers of imagery were unable to
make the fine distinctions between sensory qualities required by his
system.

Synesthesias are not usually bi-directional. For example, a person who experiences color when he hears sounds probably does not
hear sounds when he sees color. Visual-to-auditory synesthesia
(things seen accompanied by sounds) are comparatively common,
while auditory-to-visual synesthesia (having visual images upon
hearing sounds) are rare.[2] (Lyrical musical selections written specifically to arouse visual imagery, such as "Rhapsody in Blue" or
"Grand Canyon Suite" are exceptions to this.) Hallucinogenic
drugs such as LSD and mescaline increase the occurrence of synesthesias even among people who do not ordinarily experience
them. Hypnotic suggestion can also produce transformations from
one sense modality to another.[3]

While debates have raged as to whether imagery "exists" and is
useful to thinking, the concept of synesthesia has rarely been at-
tacked. Yet colored hearing and musical smells are obvious examples of sensory thinking. The reason synesthesias have not been
questioned is that they are regarded as odd or exceptional states,
much like someone being an idiot savant. However, the rarity of
this phenomenon is open to question. It is like imagery in its grada-
tions. Synesthesias are the tip of the iceberg in terms of representing consciously what most people experience preconsciously. The
evidence for this comes from several sources. First, the ease with

which synesthesias can be produced through hypnosis or psyche-delic drugs suggests that the capacity is available. Second, direct questions will reveal consistent patterns of cross-modality associa-tions in individuals. Third, and most significant, is that detailed in-terviews do not reveal a clear line between verbal associations and sensory images. Many images are so weak and ephemeral that they are hardly worthy of the name, and many associations possess sen-sory overtones. Synesthesias represent the vivid, conscious pres-ence of images that most people will experience only as verbal as-sociations.

There has not been much research into training people to control their synesthesias. The question remains whether it would be worthwhile. Is there any value of pleasure to be gained from musi-cal seeing or colored hearing? The mnemonist S., whose mental life was replete with synesthesias, occasionally found them annoy-ing, but admitted that they assisted his recall. Most of the accounts by people with synesthesias express the same ambivalence. Cross-modality sensations are helpful sometimes but distracting at other times. Ideally, people should be able to turn on their synesthesias when they are pleasurable and useful and switch them off when they are distracting. None of the reported instances of synesthesia, as far as I know, suggests this degree of mastery. However, such control is characteristic of cross-modality *associations*. Most every-one can *associate* colors to sounds and numbers to music when asked to do so, and there is a great consistency among the re-sponses. The educational system requires a tight control over associ-ative processes. The student must be able to think about American history at 9 A.M., music at 10 A.M., and first aid and physical edu-cation at 11.

Color associations are more common for some items than for others. Among British college students questioned specifically about this, the most frequent spontaneous color associations were to months of the year ("September makes me think of green, De-cember suggests white, January gray"). The next most common as-sociations were to the days of the week ("Sunday seems to go with black, Monday with white, and lucky Friday with green") and then numbers, proper names, and seasons, in that order. These color associations were more frequent among women than among men.[4] It should be noted that the associations were spontaneous. Had the researcher specifically requested the student to link, for example, months with colors, almost all would have been able to comply and there would have been even more consistency in their replies.

The new field of experimental esthetics is attempting to define these associations so that they may be put to practical use. Knowing which colors are warm and which are cool, which sounds are sharp and which are dull, which movements are threatening and which are reassuring has many practical applications in design. Only rarely do these cross-modality transfers operate consciously at a sensory level. Few people genuinely smell colors and feel numbers or become warm when certain musical notes are played, and most of us are aware of such relationships only at a symbolic level. Frequently the pairings are made on the basis of past experience, such as blue being associated with water and cold, and red with fire and heat. The pairings may be metaphorical, such as an arrow pointing upward meaning success and an arrow pointing downward meaning failure. Studies have indicated that such pairings extend beyond the boundaries of particular societies. Australian aborigines will pair the works of modern composers such as Bartok with jagged lines and Brahms with rounded contours and will match sharp odors with sharp lines and dull odors with straight lines.

Reds, yellows, and oranges tend to be more active and to "reach out" to the observer, in contrast to greens and blues, which are "receding colors." However, this does not hold for all hues or intensities. The fluorescent hues, for example, behave very differently from ordinary colors. Tempo will also affect hue. Very rapid movement creates a colorless blur. A mixture of complementary hues rotated at high speed on a color wheel produces gray. As life speeds up, either because we move faster or the word moves faster or both, it loses color and dimensionality.[5]

Studies of color symbolism in other cultures often turn up paradoxical results that can be resolved at a deeper level. Yi-Fu Tuan discusses the diverse symbolism of red and how it fits together. In China, red is used in weddings because of its association with life and joy. On the other hand, a red sky suggests warfare and disaster. At a deeper level, there is no contradiction—red is the color of blood and blood is necessary for life, but spilt blood means death. The white that means purity and cleanliness can also mean sterility, emptiness, and death.[6] How colors are perceived in different cultures makes intriguing reading. The same red color that Americans find so pleasing on Old Glory may seem harsh and jarring when seen on the Soviet flag. Of all the colors, Tuan believes that white, black, and red have the most universal significance because they are associated with products of the body whose discharge, emission, or creation is accompanied by a heightened state of emotion. Specifically, white is associated with semen and milk, red with blood, and black with excreta.

Geographer W. H. Nault suggests that children's errors in map reading are often due to faulty color associations. The youngster who uses the conventional symbolism of blue–water, yellow–sun, and red–fire will apply these to the geographic map.[7] Most mapmakers have the good sense to color water blue and the polar ice cap white, but some of the other hues make no sense. I have a popular world atlas that follows a different color system. The country that is the focus of interest is white and all the other land is tan. My immediate impression of an all-white United States is that it is a very cold country. The borders between adjacent states are outlined in pastel colors suggesting geographic barriers at all boundary crossings. Although a sophisticated reader can penetrate this code, existing associations still affect one's interpretations. The Soviet Union looks equally cold on the map of Asia when it is stark white and all the other countries are tan and the water blue. The map-dependent person also expects to find lines at the border between states and nations, and thinks of rivers not as water but as squiggly lines.

The linkage between colors and directions has been the subject of historical and philosophical investigation. In ancient Tibet, north was yellow, south was blue, east was white, and west was red. In Ireland, north was represented by black, south by white, east by purple, and west by a dun color.[8] The most complete list of these pairings of colors and directions is found in *The Symbol*

Sourcebook, by Henry Dreyfuss.[9] Following the suggestion of my colleague Stephen Jett—that associations of color and directions also existed in the United States—Marina Estabrook and I began a series of investigations on this topic.[10] The question proved to be far more complex than we had first anticipated. Rather than making a single study aimed at seeing if specific colors were associated with specific directions, we undertook ten separate investigations over a period of five years. The association between colors and directions bears significance for architects and designers, part of whose job it is to make it easy for people to find their way around. If there are common associations between a directional axis (e.g., vertical–horizontal or left–right) and a particular color, it would be useful to capitalize upon this rather than to develop purely arbitrary coding schemes.

Study 1: Colors Associated to Directions
(97 students)

The experimenter stood at the front of the room and displayed seven color charts (R, G, B, Y, Black, W, Gray). After telling the students that this was a survey designed to test their associations between colors and directions, the experimenter read out the four cardinal directions, and each time the student indicated a color association on a sheet of paper. The results showed that north was paired with the cool colors and south with the warm colors, with no clear trend for east or west.

Study 2: Intermediate Colors and Intermediate Directions
(156 students)

Our feeling was that the use of the seven colored charts might have constrained the responses. We also wanted to see how the intermediate compass points (NE, NW, SE, SW) would be rated. With another large class of students, the experimenter followed the previous procedure except that no colored charts were used. Instead the students were asked to write down the color that seemed to go with each direction. For the cardinal directions, the omission of the seven colored charts did not make much difference. North was still paired with white and blue, south with the warmer colors (red and yellow), east with green, and west with blue. The intermediate compass points reflected a mixture of associations to the cardinal directions. Northeast was paired with green, blue, and purple; the northwest with green; the southeast with green, yellow, and orange; and the southwest with brown, orange, red,and yellow. There was much more use of hybrid colors in relation to the intermediate compass points. Purple was used only five times with the cardinal directions, but forty-five times with the intermediate points. Blue-green and turquoise were never paired with the cardinal directions, but were used twenty-two times for the intermediate points. Tan and beige were used only once with the cardinal directions but twenty-one times with the intermediate points. The fact that intermediate directions produce mixed colors supports the thesis that colors and directions are linked in semantic space.

Study 3: Perceptual Images (127 students)

While the earlier studies established a relationship between directions and colors, its basis was not yet clear. One possibility was that the students' replies reflected the colors used on geographers' maps. We therefore took a new group of students and asked them to write down "the first image that comes to mind" for each of the cardinal directions. Nothing was specified about color or any other perceptual attribute. After the images had been written down, the student was asked to go back and indicate the dominant color of the image.

The replies made it clear that we were indeed dealing with pictures of real places rather than with map projections. The vast majority of images were geographic. People thought of south primarily in terms of a place and only secondarily in terms of a culture or political situation. The replies also help clarify some of the unusual responses we had obtained earlier. The most frequent images of north were snow, cold, ice, skiing, and Eskimos. Such images had white as the dominant color (62 respondents). However, 39 students associated north with forests, mountain ranges, and pine

The Mind's Eye

trees, the streams and wildlife of northern California, Oregon, Washington, and Canada. For them, the dominant color was green. Eight responses showed a blue image; 3 of these were based on lakes and 3 on the sky, while 2 other people associated north with the freeway signs of Interstate 5! Five people saw the dominant color of north as gray (the Oregon sea coast on a foggy day, the wind blowing strongly, a cold place under a gray sky). Three had a brown image of north (South Dakota, the Yukon and Alaska, the highways toward Oregon). These responses make it clear that we are dealing with images of real places, many with personal significance for the respondents.

Study 4: Regional Differences (164 students)

Since the directional images were related to specific places, it seemed logical that there would be regional differences in the meaning of north, south, east, and west. In California, east would mean the desert of Nevada and Arizona, while in Ohio it would mean the crowded, industrial eastern seaboard. We therefore repeated the association procedure of Study 2 with comparable classes at Richmond College (in Staten Island, New York City) and Louisiana State University. The results confirmed our impression of regional differences. For the California students, the dominant association to west was blue (the ocean); for the New York students, it was green; and for the Louisiana students, it had the decided brownish cast of Texas. South was associated by the California students with red and yellow and by the New York students with red, green, and yellow, but the main association for the Louisiana students was green. Since I had visited Louisiana at the time the questionnaires were administered and observed lush plant growth everywhere, the green association was understandable.

Study 5: Transivity: Association of Directions to Colors (343 students)

One important aspect of associative pairings is that they don't always operate as two-way streets. A common association to *horse* is shoe, but the reverse is not true. One cannot therefore assume that the color associations to directions are identical to the directional associations to color. We also wanted to assess the color associations of other spatial dimensions, such as top, middle, and bottom, and right, left, and center. To answer these questions, the experimenter tested another large class. The color charts were still used, but this time, instead of beginning with directions and asking for colors, the experimenter read out the seven color names and asked for spatial associations. Five different instructional sheets were circulated randomly and a student filled out only one type. The various instructions asked a student to associate the color with:

Form 5a. The words *north, south, east,* or *west.*
Form 5b. A round circle indicating compass points N, S, E, and W.
Form 5c. Right, center, or left.
Form 5d. Top, middle, or bottom.
Form 5e. Small arrows pointing left, right, up, or down.

Form 5a: Associating from Colors (100 students)

Most of the chromatic colors (red, green, blue, yellow) were paired with west, white was strongly associated with north, and black with south. One of the major differences between this and the earlier procedure is in the frequency of achromatic responses. Associating from directions to colors, very few students associated any direction with black. However, if they are asked specifically which direction goes with black, a strong black-south bond is evident.

Form 5: Compass Points Associated with Colors (61 students)

These students made their responses using compass points rather than words, this change made virtually no difference. Chromatic colors were again paired with west, white with north, and south with black.

Form 5c: (51 students)

People were asked whether a color went with right, center, or left. White was associated with the center. The chromatic colors, with the exception of blue, were rarely put at the left.

Form 5d: (51 students)

As the experimenter read out a color name, each student indicated whether it went with top, middle, or bottom. Chromatic colors were associated with the top, white with both the middle and the top, and gray and black with the bottom.

Form 5e: (80 students)

Here the students were asked to associate the colors with arrows pointing left, right, up, and down. All the chromatic colors and white were associated with arrows going up; gray and black were paired with arrows going down.

Practical Implications

Geography teachers could capitalize on dominant color associations in teaching students about places and regions. If parts of maps are colored to keep them distinct, it would probably facilitate learning to follow existing linkages rather than to go against them. Architects could use familiar color associations in aiding orientation. A common complaint about large buildings is that people have difficulty finding their way around. The arbitrary use of color can hinder orientation if it taps into the wrong color associations. A standard color coding has been developed for stop-go (red-green) but none has been developed for up-down or right-left. Any such system would do well to build upon existing linkages rather than impose them arbitrarily.

Study 6: Free Associations (54 students)

Previous investigations make it clear that colors are not the primary associations to directions nor directions to colors.[11] People who are asked for the first words that come to mind when they hear *red* or *blue* do *not* respond with compass points. Since no data were available on the associations to directions (NSEW), we asked students at a local community college (who had not been tested in any of the previous studies) for the first association that came to mind for the four cardinal directions. Of the 216 individual responses, only 2 involved colors. It seems evident that the relationship between colors and directions is not immediate and primary in consciousness. When a person daydreams about the northwest, she does not see green by itself. Rather she has the image of a forest which is green as well as wet and cool. When she thinks of north, her image turns to snow, which is white, cold, quiet, soft, undulating.

Geographic Images

These studies indicate that colors and directions are related through the mediation of imagery. Our mental pictures of places include many sensory aspects. None of our respondents mentioned the colors used on road maps as a reason for a particular color association. Most explanations involved accurate albeit stereotyped color renditions of particular components such as the blue ocean, white snow, yellow desert, and so on. A number of students reported difficulty in pinning down their images to particular colors. One student saw west as mountain ranges running into the sea topped by a great sunset. He had both temporal and spatial problems in selecting a dominant color, since his mountains were green, his ocean blue, and his sunset reddish-orange.

There are many similarities and some important differences between the dominant colors of the respondents' images and their associations. While the dominant *associations* to north were white and blue, the dominant *images* were white and green. The associations to south were yellow and red, while the images were green and brown. Associations frequently deal with stereotypes which are made according to the principle of contrast rather than similarity. This is a major difference between imagery and association. Rarely is the image of something the exact opposite of it. Yet this is frequently true of associations. Things are frequently defined in school by what they are not or with reference to their opposite numbers. One's immediate verbal association to *unattractive* is probably going to be *attractive,* and to *undecided* it may be *decided,* but one's *image* of *unattractive* will be a dowdy person and of *undecided* will be someone scratching his head or grimacing.

Association by opposition indicates a nonperceptual attitude. The tendency toward negative associations is embedding itself more insidiously in our language. During our breakfast in a restaurant in Kansas, the waitress asked my wife whether she wanted cream with her coffee. Barbara replied that she did, and the waitress delivered a little round container whose label read, "ultra pasturized nondairy product for coffee." As the reader can undoubtedly see, a non-anything doesn't produce much of an image.

Some of the differences in thinking style between visualizers and verbalizers may be traced back to the difference between image and association. Upon hearing a word, a visualizer may have a picture of what the item is, while the verbalizer has an association of what it is *not.* This may give the verbalizer the appearance of being critical and negative and quibbling about definitions rather than of dealing with situations as they are. Using colors as an illustration makes the differences between image and association easier to understand. The dominant *association* to *black* is white but the dominant *image* of *black* is darkness or night. Thus the person who reacts with a verbal association will respond differently to a stimulus than a person who responds using imagery. It is a mistake to believe that the only difference between visualizers and verbalizers is the mode in which information is processed. The very content of something seen or heard will be affected by whether it is processed through association or imagery.

13

What I Have Learned from Designers

To try to establish an island of visual literacy in an ocean of blindness is ultimately self-defeating.

(RUDOLPH ARNHEIM)

I have worked collaboratively with architects for almost twenty years. Every project on which I have worked has changed me personally and professionally. Like most nondesigners who have been involved in some capacity with the planning of buildings, I have been saddened by the fragmentation of the design professions into separate warring factions, that is, the rivalry between architects and engineers, between architects and interior designers, between city planners and landscape architects, and so on. I prefer to use the term *designer* in the generic sense to describe all those who mold space indoors and outdoors, plan neighborhoods and cities, and create new products and displays. Visualization is important to all these endeavors. Whether one is designing a housing development, a hotel interior, a store window display, or landscaping a schoolyard, the ability to picture the outcome in the mind's eye is indispensable.

If I had worked with engineers as closely as I have with designers, I would be a very different psychologist today. Above all, this collaboration has increased my visual literacy. In graduate school, most of my learning was conceptual rather than perceptual, and the major realities were the printed page and the keyboard of a calculator. In this atmosphere, I allowed my visual imagery to atrophy and forgot how to express myself graphically. This neglect became apparent in my work with architects. I can trace my interest in photography and renewed interest in painting directly to a team effort to design an island resort in Fiji. There were seven of us involved, including two architects and an architecture student, a city planner, a graphics designer, an engineer, and myself. All but the engineer and I sketched the island before trying to design anything. When it came time to prepare a brochure for the investors, the team leader collected the photographs we had also taken in preparation for the actual design work. It was painfully obvious that although my pictures of the tropical island might interest my friends and family, they were totally unsuitable for a prospectus. I quickly realized how little I knew about using a camera professionally. My earlier books had relied exclusively on text—no pictures or drawings. Most of my recent books have included pictures, and I recently finished a book on murals and a children's book on sidewalks which were primarily visual. I would not have become so deeply involved in photography without the example of my architect-friends, who never travel anywhere without a camera.

An interest in photography, however, is not always indicative of a good visual memory. Some photographers employ a good sense of composition and photographic technique mnemonics that substitute for a good visual memory. Why bother trying to retain a clear image of a scene when one can capture it on film and retain it indefinitely? Too many tourists view the world through their cameras, putting their energies into taking pictures rather than seeing what is there. I would not deny the value of visual mnemonics. A two-dimensional print can release a flow of lively three-dimensional images when one approaches it with an imaginative attitude. The issue becomes one of whether photographs are used as a substitute for visual memory or a stimulus to it or both. The kinds of pictures a person takes provide a partial answer. Are the slides suggestive, inviting, made to engage interest and exploration, or are they designs—informative and proportioned, but without sensuality and dimensionality? That architects do not see the flow of space the way other people do is reflected in the photographs they take. Buildings are shown from unusual angles, and details that most people would overlook are highlighted and exaggerated. Such pictures are intended to arouse imagery and not to substitute for it.

I regret having let my imagery decline during my school years. This has been a distinct handicap in discussions with designers who can create buildings in imagination while I must use paper or a model. Imagery permits an architect to work from plans which look flat to me no matter how hard I try to add a third dimension. On design review panels, a person's ability to make constructive comments often depends on his or her degree of visualization. Realization of this has permitted me to facilitate communication between designers, who operate as though everyone shared their capacity for visualization, and others, who require scale models or at least photographs before they can make informed decisions.

New graphic aids are making it easier for designers to present their ideas to clients with more realism. Landscape planners at Berkeley have developed a large environmental simulator. It uses scale models of urban areas or natural landscapes seen through a remotely guided periscope with a tiny movable lens ($^1/_{10}$-inch radius). Supported by a gantry and control system, the periscope can "fly," "walk," or "drive" through models of buildings or landscapes. The lens can project images onto closed-circuit television, videotape, or movie film. During its journeys, the periscope can look in any direction and can follow different routes at any desired speed. The simulator is currently being used in a study of development in San Francisco. The simulator enables neighborhood residents to examine the visual impact of proposed buildings and compare alternatives.[1]

Not all simulation procedures are as elaborate as this. At the University of Tennessee, Alton DeLong has been using inexpensive cardboard scale models to investigate people's response to buildings. He believes there is an optimal scale of about twelve-to-one that makes a model seem most realistic. A larger-than-life model would be useless and wasteful, but if the model is too small, people have difficulty putting themselves inside and moving around. I have problems visualizing a building from blueprints, but found it easy to get into DeLong's cardboard model and comment on the flow and feel of space. People's placement of plastic dolls on scale furniture produced results similar to the distances real people used in normal conversation.[2]

Jerome Sirlin of Cornell University has developed a technique for combining slides to produce composite images. Colored filters permit a client to see how a room interior would look in a different color scheme and with a different level of illumination. Various landscape solutions can be added, using slides—inserting hedges, different kinds of trees, flowers, rocks, or other natural materials. The system involves two slides projected through cardboard masks to delete unwanted portions, and then taking a photograph of the composite. The technique permits unusual combinations, such as superimposing a classroom over a garden or a library with a museum to see how the two physical structures will fit together. Many of the composite images are startling and surprising. It becomes possible to visualize a shopping center on top of a Roman bath as an exciting new concept. The technique is intended to allow designers to present ideas to clients more quickly and realistically than with conventional sketches.[3]

In the hands of a talented designer, all these methods can be valuable tools. One must, however, be aware of the important difference between toys, tools, and crutches. A toy is something to enjoy, to play with, but not to take seriously. Simulation exercises can generate student interest, break classroom routine, and otherwise liven things up without doing anything beyond that. They may also serve as tools to extend human capabilities or as crutches to restore an impaired level of functioning back to a normal, healthy condition. When it comes to visualization, designers need tools and the rest of us nondesigners can benefit more from training and practice in visualization than from tools, toys, or crutches. To the extent that models, slides, and sketches awaken imagery and increase the realism of the design process, they are welcome additions. To the extent that they substitute for visual thinking and increase people's dependence on external, prepackaged images, they work against the interests of responsive, creative design. In the hands of the talented writer, words can be as evocative as pictures, even more so when they engage the imagination of the reader to create internal pictures. Good architectural writing can place the reader inside a building, over it, around it, enabling one to experience it with all senses operating. One of the most useful aspects of imagery is this ability to picture scenes from unusual angles. This can mean zooming into a building and looking at rooms and buildings from the inside out. This ability can be put to practical use, for instance, in designing a kindergarten or children's playground where surfaces, textures, and distances fit the child's scale. This is not accomplished simply by reducing everything 40 percent in size, as the abstract thinker might imagine, but by perceptually exploring the area from a child's vantage point and deciding which spaces are friendly and cozy and which are exposed and threatening.

The ability to mentally project oneself into and out of buildings and to float in space can be misused. Architects often create stylized sketches of buildings from odd angles with the main features exaggerated. This technique can be deceitful and self-serving when the architect selects an elevation and angle from which the building looks best rather than showing the way people will typically see it. I have come to feel a little more comfortable about the exaggeration of critical features in sketches. Superfeatures, as Kristina Hooper calls them, orient us in space and help us find our way about.[4] In many respects, the stylized distortions of the architect's drawings are closer than literal renditions or photographs to the way people remember buildings. This is not, of course, true of all schematic drawings. Sometimes the architect's conception of what is important or memorable bears no relationship to how people actually see a building. However, the principle of exaggerating distinctive features, which is routinely employed in schematic drawing, generally has a valid basis in architectural imagery.

Architects share with other spatially minded people a difficulty in communicating with people who think in linear terms. Psychotherapist Rosemary Gordon was concerned about the large amount of acrimony and personal feuding among her friends in the British art world. How is it, she asked herself, that these intelligent, talented musicians, artists, designers, and filmmakers could get so angry with one another so often? Instead of seeking the answer in long-buried childhood experiences, Gordon surmised that the source of much of the discord was the unique, vivid image world of the creative person. When an architect's image of a design is clear and compelling, it is difficult for him or her to believe that other people do not share it. The same is true of the stage designer with an intense, unequivocal image of how the set should appear. Gordon calls this "the arrogant certainty" of creative people. A stage designer of her acquaintance expressed anger and resentment when his stagehands could not execute his designs quickly and easily. Though his image was clear and striking to himself, he had difficulty sharing it verbally with others. Another stage designer described his joy when his workers were able to interpret his instructions properly. When this happened, it seemed miraculous to him, almost like a telepathic communication.[5]

Several times previously, I have discussed the problems that arise when visualizers talk with verbalizers. Sadly, the problems can be just as severe when visualizers talk to one another and neither is able to adequately describe his or her personal conception yet believes it to be the proper one. And not all creative people are visually gifted. Some novelists and playwrights, particularly those of a philosophical bent, seem more verbal than visual. Gordon found that those musicians with extensive early contact with opera tended to visualize while listening to music, while musicians whose backgrounds lay primarily in instrumental music downgraded the visual aspects of the experience. Early exposure as well as subsequent practice will bias a creative person toward one sense modality and away from another. Two photographers taking pictures of a sunset will visualize the scene differently if one works in black and white and the other in color. The still photographer and the movie photographer will also be imagining the same event in different idioms—the one as a succession of single shots and the other as an ongoing event. The attempt to explain communication problems in the arts on the basis of cognitive style seems far more productive than dismissing some artists as immature and emotional. A positive feature of imagery research is that it takes each person's view of the world seriously. Artists, like all people, act on the basis

Husband and wife have different images of their dream house. The architect has his image, too.

of their perceptions, and perceptions must be shared in any sort of collaborative work. Possibly because we live in a society that puts a high premium on individualism, cooperative work has become extraordinarily difficult and painful for many people. So often it seems that the most creative, intelligent, and motivated men and women are prima donnas who cannot work effectively with others.

Design today *is* a collaborative effort. A product designer must take into account not only consumer preferences but also the situation of the manufacturer and issues of packaging, transportation, and marketing. When an architect has responsibility for a building, there are likely to be consultants from fields as diverse as civil engineering, sewage disposal, transportation planning, and finance providing inputs as well. Architecture, like other design fields, requires visualizers who can talk with verbalizers. Without this, there is only the hermetic model of architecture as a field where architects design buildings for one another. There are some traces of this in the awards system as well as in the mythology of *The Fountainhead,* whose hero remains faithful to his internal image no matter what the client wants.[6] Fortunately, architecture students today are being taught that if they want to build their visions, they will have to share them with clients, bankers, construction workers, and government officials.

The city planners I have encountered do not seem as visual as architects. Many seem to be distinctly conceptual types with weak imagery. This is no handicap in those aspects of their work which have to do with codes, variances, and zoning. Indeed, much of the work of contemporary planning is closer to law than design. The term *planner* itself may be a misnomer, since most of these people review plans submitted by others rather than doing original designs themselves. The computer has been proposed as a substitute for visual imagery in creating the cityscape. With the proper instructions, a computer can supply a view of a building or neighborhood from any point or elevation. This sounds like more of an advance than it actually is. A computer is not very skilled artistically and its drawings are crude, stiff, and stereotyped.

So often it seems that public buildings intended to welcome people contain hard, unreflecting surfaces that reverberate sound throughout the halls and corridors to make conversation difficult. In his book *Experiencing Architecture,* Steen Eiler Rasmussen asks, "Can architecture be heard? Most people would probably say that as architecture does not produce sound, it cannot be heard. But neither does it radiate light, and yet it can be seen. We see the light it reflects and thereby gain an impression of form and material. In the same way we hear the sounds it reflects and they, too, give us an impression of form and material. Differently shaped rooms and different materials reverberate differently." [7]

A building will be viewed most often by people who are in motion, either along an adjacent street or through its interior. Architect Philip Thiel has spent over a decade developing a language of spatial experience. Like the music notation system, it enables one to design sequential experiences rather than static monuments. Even when a viewer remains stationary and gazes at a building, his senses are picking up the relationship between the building and neighborhood and sky, noises from traffic, and people walking by, and a continuous flow of movements in, out, and across. [8]

In a design review session, when someone suggests moving the proposed location of a building, people have to mentally shift the model around and make the connections between the small cubes and the neighborhood. I have frequently found myself "faking it" during such sessions, as my powers of visualization are not as good as those of designers in imagining how the building will look when the little cube is moved from *A* to *B*. In such situations, I have felt somewhat akin to a blind man among the sighted. I was not totally useless, merely handicapped.

Because they can visualize their creations vividly and effortlessly, most architects regard their models primarily as devices for helping the client, the general public, or city authorities see what the building will look like. The extent of the viewers' visual capabilities becomes especially critical when a model is intended to represent a tentative scheme subject to modification. The future occupants of a building should be active in proposing changes at the planning stage rather than being limited to reactive statements of like and dislike once the structure is built. If we take seriously the idea of involving people in the design of their houses, work places, neighborhoods, and cities, their level of sensory literacy must be increased. With the aid of models and diagrams, they should be able to project themselves into a setting and experience it in all their sense modalities.

Even good visualizers may not use their imagery if the situation discourages it. Imagine a college class of music students sitting in a lecture hall listening to selections played on a phonograph. The students are told that they are going to be tested later on a multiple-choice examination. Many students will spend their time coding the music into verbal categories of period, style, and composer rather than listening. In a similar way, a city planner taking a group of students for a tour of the city can inadvertently produce the same kind of computerlike storage into abstract categories. Architects, as members of one of the few professions to escape this pattern of verbal dominance, have a special responsibility to share the benefits of visual literacy. To accomplish this, though, they will first have to recognize that other people think differently than they. This fact should be evident both in immediate perception—other people's observations and responses being less finely tuned to the environment—and in the way information is stored by other people. The differences between visualizers and verbalizers are even more significant in memory than in perception. It will be extraordinarily difficult for an architect to teach environmental literacy to someone who lacks sensory memory. Obviously, the solution is to raise the general level of sensory memory first. It is time to discard Galton's original analogy of the anoptic individual as totally blind. Total blindness in most cases is unchangeable. A lack of imagery is correctable through training. There may be a few brain-damaged individuals who totally lack the capacity for sensory thought, but for all others, the capacity is undeveloped rather than absent.

The molding of form is one of the most satisfying human activities. Its origins are as ancient as the quests for shelter, for protection, and for visual beauty. The process can begin with play (a good motive for beginning any activity), but it will eventually progress to intentional design. That does not mean each generation has to begin anew to reconstruct the physical environment. There is much to be said for the Native American attitudes of adaptation and "fittingness," of passing through places as a fish swims through water. This idea is not inconsistent with deliberate and intentional design. The patterns of life and physical artifacts of native culture—products of design and construction—were in harmony with the landscape. In our age, too, good design must involve harmony with nature, including human nature and its need for open space and greenery. When people develop greater visual sensitivity, professional designers will not be put out of business. On the contrary, as people begin actively seeing what is around them, the talents and services of designers will be in greater demand. Visual *il*literacy, not visual literacy, is the threat to good design. The task of raising the level of visual thinking in our society becomes an important part of design practice. The dream is this: every person a designer; every designer an educator; every educator a practitioner.

No one in this society can escape the effects of the design professions. Architecture is inescapable even if it affects us mostly from beyond our immediate awareness. The thinking style of designers is therefore a matter of great practical importance. I am grateful to my architect friends for all they have taught me, not only about how they think, but about how I think myself. I have no desire to become an architect myself. I believe that I can make a more meaningful contribution to society and also to the design fields as a psychologist. Interdisciplinary collaboration does not mean the disappearance of separate professions or thinking styles but the recognition that each has something special to contribute. What I have learned from architects has made me a better psychologist. When I taught classes fifteen years ago, I did not use a single illustration. Today I use some kind of graphic material in almost every lecture. An image of a person who is terribly depressed or experiencing delirium tremens makes these conditions more tangible and meaningful. Their names are no longer mere labels, but words that describe real people who are hurting.

Since I have become aware of the importance of imagery in learning, I try to link up what I teach to the students' personal experiences. I do not want psychology to become another foreign language. I am not averse to introducing students to new concepts or to different ways of looking at behavior, so long as there is some connection between what is new and what they already know. The typical alcoholic may be an abstraction that has never existed in a person's real life, but at any given moment there are tens of thousands of destitute and homeless men and women on the skid rows of American cities and millions of closest alcoholics in the bedrooms and board rooms of America who will cause innumerable traffic accidents and deaths every year. The tangibility of these people and events must be included in the subject matter of the course. If students emerge knowing a vocabulary and set of facts without being able to connect them to their lives and to the outside world, then I have failed as a teacher. To the extent that my lectures have become more visual and imageable, I will give a large portion of the credit for this to my association with architects and designers.

It seems fitting to end this book with a tribute to the profession that sensitized me most keenly to the creative uses of visual thinking. The basis of effective collaboration in any field is respect for the different ways that others think. These differences are rarely as striking as those between the researcher R. and the mnemonist S. If they were, I probably would not have felt it necessary to write this book. Most of the time, the differences between visualizers and verbalizers go unrecognized—a wife is puzzled at her husband's inability to describe the features of someone he has just met, a teacher is frustrated when a student doesn't think in a linear fashion, a couple is unable to see from blueprints what their new house is going to look like, your friend invites you to his cabin for the weekend but cannot explain to you how to get there, or two engineers work side by side in the same office, but the first sees a project in its totality in the mind's eye, while the second will not believe anything until the calculations check out on paper. These are but a few examples; they are obvious, but are so often accepted as part of the miscommunications of life that they go unrecognized as the results of dramatically different styles of thinking.

Until I began working with architects, most of my associates were verbalizers like myself. The architects with whom I have worked have tended to be good imagers—often very good—but not superimagers. I have never come across any who could do the Elizabeth trick of mentally combining two thousand-dot patterns or two disparate art figures into a meaningful whole. Faced with two partial figures, neither of which makes sense, even the visual person proceeds analytically. I have found very good imagers among architects who tried to combine the two parts through cross-referencing or matching the pieces. Based on an initial hunch as to what the combined figure might be, they select particular lines to move and then check them for meaningfulness in the new position. If that doesn't work, the line will be replaced and another line moved. This is a completely novel task for most people. Even good imagers usually have no experience or training in superimposing one incomplete figure on another. When the initial strategy of visual problem solving does not succeed, the person may switch to an analytic mode and attempt to reconstruct the figures on a piecemeal basis. Unlike S., these architects are not singleminded thinkers. Switching is an important part of their lives. When one mode of thinking does not succeed, they are willing and able to try another. Switching implies the capability of combining synthesis and analysis, creating a whole figure and then examining each of the parts in the context of the totality. Because of the nature of our educational system, one frequently comes across visualizers who solve intellectual problems in a nonvisual way. They have the capacity and the inclination to organize information spatially but avoid doing this in "serious work." But often such a basically visual person does not feel comfortable using an analytical approach, either. The result may be a ritualistic abstraction, fuzzy at the edges as the excluded images try to gain entrance.

Finally

Scientists have found that the tastes, smells, and visual impressions of the past can be revived through stimulation of certain parts of the brain. These sensory memories never leave us completely, but they are lost to consciousness. Sensory memory is the capacity to recall the stuff of experience and to use it creatively. This includes the capacity to develop novel combinations, which is the basis of design. When designs are created without regard to the senses, the result is likely to be a somber, rayless, joyless world dominated by euphemism and word magic where categories are more important than experience, where everything appears to be and seems to be, but nothing is, no one feels. The most common complaint of people seeking psychotherapy is not hysteria, as it was in Freud's day, but detachment from experience. People complain that they don't feel anything, not even their own existence. The decline in sensory thinking is an important part of this. Fortunately, this deficit is remediable. Adults can, through proper exercise and training, develop evocative memories and increase the pungency and richness of imagination. For children, the problem is how to let them retain the capacity for imagery and carry it into adult life.

Working with architects made it easy to recognize the utility of visualization in the fine arts and applied arts, but as I came to learn more about it and to connect visual thinking with taste, touch, sound, smell, and motor imagery, its role in enriching experience became apparent. Sensory memory is not the esoteric skill of a few oddball artists, composers, and wine tasters. Their abilities represent only the upper end of the spectrum of talents much more widely distributed.

Most people think about imagery in connection with the arts, particularly the visual arts. For some time, I thought of imagery mostly in connection with design, particularly architecture. Now I think of it in relation to the quality of life, the enjoyment of experience, and the possession of richer and more sensual memories. Imagery helps to keep us closer to experience, to our bodies, to one another, and to nature. The technical aspects of design, like the factual aspects of memory, can be produced efficiently by a computer—but design with delight, design with a glow, cannot. That is where the human capacity to conjure in the mind's eye becomes necessary.

Notes

Chapter 1

1. Francis Galton, *Inquiries into Human Faculty and its Development* (London: Dent, 1907).
2. Robert Gerard, *Psychosynthesis: A Psychotherapy for the Whole Man,* Publication No. 14 of the Psychosynthesis Research Foundation, 1964.
3. William James, *Psychology* (Cleveland: World Publishing Co., 1948).
4. Ray H. Stetson, "Types of Imagination," *Psychological Review* 3 (1896): 398–411.
5. Quoted in "Points to Ponder," *Reader's Digest,* Jan. 1976, p. 181.
6. Henry Miller, *Book of Friends* (Santa Barbara, Calif.: Capra Press, 1976), p. 9.
7. Roy Andries De Groot, *Handbook for Hosts* (New York: Grosset & Dunlap, 1973), p. 4.
8. Edwin A. Kirkpatrick, *Imagination and its Place in Education* (Boston: Ginn and Co., 1920).
9. G. H. Bower, "Analysis of a Mnemonic Device," *American Scientist* 58 (1970): 496–516.
10. Gardner Murphy, *Personality* (New York: Harper, 1947), p. 989.
11. Peter McKeller, *Imagination and Thinking* (New York: Basic Books, 1957), pp. 136–37.

12. Fernando A. Fleites, "Imagery: An Experimental and Experiential Analysis" (Senior Project, York College of CUNY, 1976).
13. Isaac Asimov, *Is Anyone There?* (Garden City, New York: Doubleday, 1967), p. 18.
14. Diana Macknown, "Louise Nevelson: A Great Artist Who Knew What She Wanted and Got It," *Mademoiselle,* Sept. 1976, p. 225.

Chapter 2

1. Carl L. Schleich, *Vom Schaltwerk Der Gedunken* (Frankfurt: Fischer Verlag, 1919).
2. David C. Rimm and Jil Bottrell, "Four Measures of Visual Imagination," *Behavioral Research and Therapy* 7 (1969): 63–69. See also J. Grossberg and H. Wilson, "Physiological Changes Accompanying Imagined Fear Situations." (Paper read at Western Psychological Association Meetings, San Francisco, May 1967.)
3. A. R. Luria, *The Mind of a Mnemonist* (New York: Basic Books, 1968).
4. David F. Marks, "Individual Differences in the Vividness of Visual Imagery and Their Effect on Function," in P. W. Sheenhan, *The Function and Nature of Imagery* (New York: Academic Press, 1972), pp. 83–108.
5. J. B. Juhasz, "Imagining, Imitation, and Role-Taking" (Ph.D. diss. University of California, Berkeley, 1969).
6. L. V. Clark, "Effect of Mental Practice on the Development of a Certain Motor Skill," *Research Quarterly* 31 (1960): 560–69.
7. I am indebted to Stephen Goldfinger for making available to me his excellent review of research on mental rehearsal.
8. R. A. Bandell, R. A. Davis, and H. A. Clugston, "The Function of Mental Practice in the Acquisition of Motor Skills," *Journal of General Psychology* 29 (1943): 243–50.
9. W. E. Twining, "Mental Practice and Physical Practice in

Learning a Motor Skill," *Research Quarterly* 20 (1949): 432–35.

10. K. B. Start, "Kinaesthesis and Mental Practice," *Research Quarterly* 35 (1964): 316–20.

11. G. E. Powell, "Negative and Positive Mental Practice in Motor Skill Acquisition," *Perceptual and Motor Skills* 37 (1973): 312.

12. C. I. Rawlings, et al., "The Facilitating Effects of Mental Rehearsal in the Acquisition of Rotary Pursuit Tracking," *Psychonomic Science* 6 (1972): 71–73.

13. C. F. Diehl and N. C. England, "Mental Imagery," *Journal of Speech and Hearing Research* 1 (1958): 268–74.

14. Truman Capote, "Unspoiled Monsters," *Esquire,* May 1976, p. 59.

15. Bernard Berenson, *The Italian Painters of the Renaissance* (New York: Phaidon, 1952), p. 81.

16. David Vestal, "Two Ways of Photographing: Seeing Versus Visualization," *Popular Photography,* April 1976, pp. 78–79.

17. David Vestal, *The Craft of Photography* (New York: Harper and Row, 1975).

18. Ansel Adams, "My Fifty Years in Photography," *Popular Photography,* August 1973, p. 200.

19. Peter C. Bunnell, Introduction to *Jerry N. Uelsmann* (New York: Aperture Monographs, 1973).

20. Jerry N. Uelsmann, "How Jerry Uelsmann Creates his Multiple Images," *Popular Photography,* January 1977, pp. 78–85.

21. E. T. Hall, *The Silent Language* (Garden City: Doubleday, 1959).

22. Bertram D. Lewin, *The Image and the Past* (New York: International Universities Press, 1968).

Chapter 3

1. G. W. Allport, "Eidetic Imagery," *British Journal of Psychology* 15 (1924): 99–120.

2. Aristotle, *De Anima* (Hett translation), p. 432.

3. Herbert F. Crovitz, *Galton's Walk* (New York: Harper and Row, 1970), p. 5.

4. This was an extension of Lord Kelvin's dictum, "If you cannot measure it, your knowledge is meager and unsatisfactory," later parodied by economist Frank Knight, who added, "And if you can't measure it, measure it anyway." (*Saturday Review,* Feb. 21, 1976, p. 22.)

5. G. H. Betts, *The Distribution and Function of Mental Imagery* (Teachers College: Columbia University, 1909).

6. Ann Roe, "A Study of Imagery in Research Scientists," *Journal of Personality* 19 (1951): 459–70.

7. Frances A. Yates, *The Art of Memory* (Chicago: University of Chicago Press, 1966), p. 277.

8. Rudolf Arnheim, *Visual Thinking* (Berkeley: University of California Press, 1969).

9. C. T. Meyers, *Some Observation on Problem Solving in Spatial Relations Tests.* Research Bulletin RB-58-16 (Princeton, N.J.: Educational Testing Service, 1958).

10. S. J. Segal, *Imagery* (New York: Academic Press, 1971).

11. Alan Richardson, *Mental Imagery* (London: Routledge and Kegan Paul, 1969).

12. P. L. Short and W. G. Walter, "The Relationship Between Physiological Variance and Stereognosis," *EEG Clinical Neurophysiology* 6 (1954): 29–44.

13. W. G. Walter, *The Living Brain* (London: Duckworth, 1953).

14. Wilder Penfield and H. Jasper, *Epilepsy and the Functional Anatomy of the Human Brain* (Boston: Little, Brown, 1954), p. 242.

15. E. Ray John, *Mechanisms of Memory* (New York: Academic Press, 1967), p. 410.

16. W. Dement and N. Kleitman, "The Relation of Eye Movements During Sleep to Dream Activity," *Journal of Experimental Psychology* 53 (1957): 339–46.

17. Richard G. Coss, "Electro-Oculography: Drawing with the Eye," *Leonardo* 2(1969): 399–401.

18. Gary E. Schwartz, Richard J. Davidson, and Eric Pugash,

"Voluntary Control of Patterns of EEG Parietal Asymmetry," *Psychophysiology,* in press.

19. Paul Bakan, "The Right Brain is the Dreamer," *Psychology Today,* November, 1976, p. 66.

20. M. Kinsbourne, "Eye and Head Turning Indicates Cerebral Lateralization," *Science* 176 (1972): 539–41.

21. Vladislav Zikmund, "Physiological Correlates of Visual Imagery," in P. W. Sheehan, *The Function and Nature of Imagery* (New York: Academic Press, 1972), pp. 355–87.

22. R. R. Holt, "Imagery: the Return of the Ostracized," *American Psychologist* 19 (1964): 254–64.

23. R. Sommer and H. Osmond, "Autobiographies of Mental Patients," *Journal of Mental Science*, 107 (1960): 648–62.

24. Carl G. Jung, *Memories, Dreams, Reflections* (New York: Pantheon Books, 1961).

25. D. P. Shreber, *Memoirs of My Nervous Illness,* eds. Hunter and MacAlpine (London: William Dawson, 1955).

26. Albert Speer, *Spandau: The Secret Diaries* (New York: Pocket Books, 1977), pp. 338–39.

27. David Marks, "Individual Differences in the Vividness of Visual Imagery and Their Effects on Function," in P. W. Sheehan, *The Function and Nature of Imagery* (New York: Academic Press, 1972), pp. 83–108.

Chapter 4

1. David Stea and J. M. Blaut, "Some Preliminary Observations on Spatial Learning in School Children," in Roger M. Downs and David Stea, eds., *Image and Environment* (Chicago: Aldine, 1973), pp. 226–34.

2. Robert H. McKim, "Visual Thinking and the Design Process," *Engineering Education,* March 1968, pp. 795–99.

3. E. R. Jaensch, *Eidetic Imagery* (London: Kegan Paul, 1930).

4. K. H. Slatter, "Alpha Rhythm and Mental Imagery," *EEG Clinical Neurophysiology,* 12 (1960): 851–59.

5. G. H. Bower, "Analysis of a Mnemonic Device," *American Scientist* 58 (1970): 496–516.

6. K. A. Wollen, "Variables that Determine the Effectiveness of Picture Mediators in Paired-Associate Learning" (Paper presented at the November, 1969, meeting of the Psychonomic Society, Saint Louis).

7. A. Paivio and H. W. Okovite, "Word Imagery Modalities and Associative Learning in Blind and Sighted Subjects," *Journal of Verbal Learning and Verbal Behavior,* 10 (1971): 506–10.

8. Marion Perlmutter and Nancy A. Myers, "Young Children's Coding and Storage of Visual and Verbal Material," *Child Development* 46(1975): 215–19.

9. J. Ross and K. A. Lawrence, "Some Observations on Memory Artifice," *Psychonomic Science,* 13 (1968): 107–18.

10. Bower, "Analysis of a Mnemonic Device."

11. R. C. Henderson and J. L. Hidde, cited in Allan Paivio, "The Role of Imagery in Learning and Memory," in P. W. Sheehan, *The Function and Nature of Imagery* (New York: Academic Press, 1972), p. 262.

12. George Atwood, "An Experimental Study of Visual Imagination and Memory," *Cognitive Psychology,* 2 (1971): 290–99.

13. Bower, "Analysis of a Mnemonic Device."

14. A. A. H. El Koussy, "The Visual Perception of Space," *British Journal of Psychology Monograph,* Supplement 20 (1935).

15. A. A. H. El Koussy, *The Direction of Research in the Domain of Spatial Aptitudes* (Paris: Editions de la Centre National de la Recherche Scientifique, 1955).

16. G. Clarke, "The Range and Nature of Factors in Perceptual Tests" (Ph.D. thesis, University of London, 1936).

17. W. B. Michael, J. P. Guilford, B. Fruchter, and W. S. Zimmerman, "The Description of Spatial-Visualization Abilities," *Educational and Psychological Measurement,* 17 (1957): 185–99.

18. I. M. Smith, *Spatial Ability* (San Diego, Calif.: Robert R. Knapp, 1964).

19. Ibid.

20. Ibid.

21. J. Leask, R. N. Haber, and R. B. Haber, "Eidetic Imagery in Children: II Longitudinal and Experimental Results," *Psychonomic Monograph,* Supplement 3 (1969).

22. A. Paivio, "Latency of Verbal Associations and Imagery to Noun Stimuli as a Function of Abstractness and Generality," *Canadian Journal of Psychology,* 20(1966): 496–516.

23. Bower, "Analysis of a Mnemonic Device."

Chapter 5

1. Lloyd F. Scott, "Increasing Mathematics Learning Through Improving Instructional Organization," in William F. Lamon, *Learning and the Nature of Mathematics* (Chicago: Science Research Associates, 1972), p. 23.

2. Seaton E. Smith, Jr., *Explorations in Elementary Mathematics* (Englewood Cliffs, N.J.: Prentice Hall, 1966), p. 11.

3. National Council of Teachers of Mathematics, *The Revolution in Teaching Mathematics* (Wash., D.C.: National Council of Teachers of Mathematics, 1961).

4. Francis J. Mueller, *Understanding the New Elementary School Mathematics* (Belmont, Calif.: Dickenson Publishing Co., 1965).

5. Donovan A. Johnson and Robert Rahtz, *The New Mathematics in Our Schools* (New York: Macmillan, 1966), p. 8.

6. B. Inhelder and J. Piaget, *The Growth of Thinking from Childhood to Adolescence* (New York: Basic Books, 1959).

7. John D. Williams, "Barriers to Arithmetical Understanding," *Mathematics Teaching* 28 (1964).

8. J. Fang, *Numbers Racket* (Port Washington, N.Y.: Kennikat Press, 1968), p. 26.

9. Jacques Hadamard, *The Psychology of Invention in the Mathematical Field* (Princeton, N.J.: Princeton University Press, 1945), p. 142.

10. Rózsa Péter, *Playing with Infinity* (New York: Dover Publications, 1975), p. xii.

11. Sloan Wilson, "Why Jessie Hates English," *Saturday Review,* September 18, 1976, pp. 11–13.

12. John Ciardi, "Ghosts in an Inscription," *Saturday Review*, August 21, 1976, p. 52.

13. Farley Mowat, *Never Cry Wolf* (New York: Dell Publishing Co., 1963), p. 9.

14. Lloyd F. Scott, *Trends in Elementary School Mathematics* (Chicago: Rand-McNally, 1966).

15. Helene Sherman, *Common Elements in New Mathematics Programs* (New York: Teachers College Press, 1972).

16. G. Cuisinaire and C. Gattegno, *Numbers in Colour*, 3rd edition (London: Heinemann, 1961).

17. Caleb Gattegno, *What We Owe Children* (New York: Outerbridge and Dienstfrey, 1970).

18. Eleanor E. Maccoby and Carol N. Jacklin, *The Psychology of Sex Differences* (Stanford, Calif.: Stanford University Press, 1974), p. 351.

19. Deborah P. Waber, "Sex Differences in Cognition: A Function of Maturational Rate?" *Science* 192 (May 7, 1976): 574–76.

20. J. Levy, *Nature* (London), 224 (1969): 614.

Chapter 6

1. E. R. Jaensch, *Eidetic Imagery* (London: Kegan Paul, 1930).

2. Ralph N. Haber, "Eidetic Images," *Scientific American,* April 1969, pp. 36–44.

3. Cynthia R. Gray and Kent Gummerman, "The Enigmatic Eidetic Image," *Psychological Bulletin,* 82 (1975): 383–407.

4. J. Leask, R. N. Haber, and R. B. Haber, "Eidetic Imagery in Children: II Longitudinal and Experimental Results," *Psychonomic Monograph,* Supplement 3 (1969): 39.

5. Charles F. Stromeyer III, "Eidetikers," *Psychology Today,* November 1970, pp. 77–80.

6. Daniel A. Pollen and Michael C. Trachtenberg, "Alpha Rhythm and Eye Movement in Eidetic Imagery," *Nature,* 237, pp. 109–112.

7. Neil S. Walker, "Restoration of Eidetic Imagery Via Hypnotic Age Regression," *Journal of Abnormal Psychology,* in press.

8. M. Parrish, R. M. Lundy, and H. W. Leibowitz, "Effect of

Hypnotic Age Regression on the Magnitude of the Ponzo and Poggendorff Illusions,'' *Journal of Abnormal Psychology,* 74, (1969): 693–98.

9. W. A. Bousfield and H. Barry, ''The Visual Imagery of a Lightning Calculator,'' *American Journal of Psychology,* 45, (1933): 353–58.

10. Fred Barlow, *Mental Prodigies* (New York: Greenwood Press, 1952).

11. Max Coltheart and Marcia J. Glick, ''Visual Imagery: A Case Study,'' *Quarterly Journal of Experimental Psychology,* 26, (1974): 438–453.

12. James Adams, *Conceptual Blockbusting* (San Francisco: W. H. Freeman, 1974).

13. A. R. Luria, *Mind of a Mnemonist* (New York: Basic Books, 1968).

14. Ibid., p. 36.

15. Ibid., p. 41.

Chapter 7

1. Simone de Beauvoir, *All Said and Done* (London: Deutsch, Weidenfeld and Nicolson, 1974).

2. Brendan Gill, *Here at the New Yorker* (New York: Random House, 1975), p. 37.

3. William James, *Psychology* (Cleveland: World Publishing Co., 1948), p. 307.

4. J. Varendonck, *The Psychology of Daydreams* (London: George Allen and Unwin, 1921), p. 57.

5. Robert H. McKim, *Experiences in Visual Thinking* (Monterey, Calif.: Brooks-Cole, 1972).

Chapter 8

1. Frances A. Yates, *The Art of Memory* (Chicago: University of Chicago Press, 1966), p. 169.

2. Ibid., p. 370.

3. J. Hastings, ed., *Encyclopedia of Religion and Ethics,* Vol. X (New York: Scribner, 1928), pp. 213–214.

4. Yates, *The Art of Memory,* p. 8.

5. Gordon Bower, "Analysis of a Mnemonic Device," *American Scientist,* 58 (1970): 496–516.

6. K. Lynch, *The Image of the City* (Cambridge, Mass.: MIT Press, 1960).

7. Paul D. Hauck, Carol C. Walsh, and Neal E. A. Kroll, "Visual Imagery Mnemonics," *Bulletin of the Psychonomic Society,* 7 (1976): 160–62.

8. R. J. Senter, *Review of Mnemonics and Mnemonotechnics for Improved Memory* (Wright-Patterson Air Force Base, Ohio: Aerospace Medical Research Laboratories, 1965).

9. Gordon Wood, "Mnemonic Systems in Recall," *Journal of Educational Psychology* 58 (1967): 1–27.

10. Victor Werner, *Shortcut Memory* (New York: Cowles Educational Corporation, 1968).

11. Harry Lorayne, *Remembering People: The Key to Success* (New York: Stein and Day, 1975).

12. George M. Stratton, "The Mnemonic Feat of the Shass Pollak," *Psychological Review* 24 (1917): 224–47.

13. Alex Haley, *Roots* (Garden City, N.Y.: Doubleday, 1976).

14. Bower, "Analysis of a Mnemonic Device."

15. George A. Miller, "Information and Memory," *Scientific American* 195 (1956): 42–46.

16. Ian M. L. Hunter, "Imagery, Comprehension, and Mnemonics," *Journal of Mental Imagery* 1 (1977): 65–72.

Chapter 9

1. Bruno Furst, *Stop Forgetting,* rev. ed. (Garden City, N.Y.: Doubleday, 1972).

2. R. J. Senter, *Review of Mnemonics and Mnemonotechnics for Improved Memory* (Wright-Patterson Air Force Base, Ohio: Aerospace Medical Research Laboratories, 1965).

3. Francis Galton, *Inquiries into Human Faculty and its Development* (London: Dent, 1907).

4. Kristina Hooper, *Imaging and Visual Thinking* (Milton Keynes, England: The Open University Press, 1976).

5. Grace Petitclerc, *The 3-D Test for Visualization Skill* (San Rafael, Calif.: Academic Therapy Publication, 1972).

6. Richard DeMille, *Children's Imagination Games* (Los Angeles: Dunbar Guidance Center, 1955).

7. Robert McKim, *Experiences in Visual Thinking* (Monterey, Calif.: Brooks-Cole, 1972).

8. R. Fischer, "The Perception-Hallucination Continuum," *Diseases of the Nervous System* 30 (1969): 161–71.

9. B. R. Bugelski, "The Definition of the Image," in *Imagery: Current Cognitive Approaches,* S. J. Segal, ed. (New York: Academic Press, 1971), p. 56.

10. Ross Parmenter, *The Awakened Eye* (Middletown, Conn.: Wesleyan University Press, 1968).

11. Edward W. Maupin, "On Meditation," in *Altered States of Consciousness,* C. T. Tart, ed. (New York: John Wiley, 1969), p. 196.

12. F. L. Golla and S. Antonovitch, "The Respiratory Rhythm in its Relation to the Mechanism of Thought," *Brain* 52 (1929): 491–509.

13. R. Morgan and P. Bakan, "Sensory Deprivation Hallucinations and Other Sleep Behaviors as a Function of Position, Method of Report, and Anxiety," *Perceptual and Motor Skills* 20 (1965): 19–25.

14. E. Berdach and P. Bakan, "Body Position and Free Recall of Early Memories," *Psychotherapy* 4 (1967): 101–102.

15. H. W. Yoxall, *The Enjoyment of Wine* (London: Michael Joseph, Ltd., 1972), p. 11.

16. Robert L. Balzer, *The Pleasures of Wine* (Indianapolis: Bobbs-Merrill, 1964), p. 19.

17. J. M. Broadbent, *Wine Tasting,* second edition (London: Christie Wine Publication, 1973).

18. G. Grazzi-Soncini, cited in R. L. Balzer, *The Pleasures of Wine,* p. 23.

19. Adrienne Lehrer, "Talking About Wine," *Language* 51 (December 1975): 887–923.

20. Balzer, *The Pleasures of Wine,* p. 26.
21. Willis H. Harman, Robert H. McKim, Robert E. Mogar, James Fadimen, and M. J. Stolaroff, "Psychedelic Agents in Creative Problem Solving: A Pilot Study," *Psychological Reports* 19 (1966): 211–227.

Chapter 10

1. Joseph E. Shorr, *Psychotherapy Through Imagery* (New York: Intercontinental Medical Book Corporation, 1974).
2. Jerome L. Singer, *Imagery and Daydream Methods in Psychotherapy and Behavior Modification* (New York: Academic Press, 1974).
3. Shorr, *Psychotherapy Through Imagery.*
4. Sigmund Freud, *The Standard Edition of the Complete Psychological Works of Sigmund Freud,* Vol. 6 (London: The Hogarth Press, 1953), p. 47.
5. Karl Abraham, "Restrictions and Transformations of Scoptophilia in Psychoneurotics," in *Selected Papers on Psychoanalysis* (London: Hogarth Press, 1953), p. 195.
6. Bertram D. Lewin, *The Image and the Past* (New York: International Universities Press, 1968).
7. Robert Gerard, *Psychosynthesis: A Psychotherapy for the Whole Man,* Publication No. 14 of the Psychosynthesis Research Foundation, 1964.
8. Roberto Assagioli, *Psychosynthesis: A Manual of Principles and Techniques* (New York: Hobbs, Dorman, 1965).
9. Wilson Van Dusen, *The Natural Depth in Man* (New York: Harper and Row, 1972).
10. J. Wolpe, *Psychotherapy by Reciprocal Inhibition* (Stanford, Calif.: Stanford University Press, 1958).
11. Donald R. Katz, "Drawing Fire," *Rolling Stone,* November 4, 1976, p. 89.
12. J. R. Cautela, "Covert Reinforcement," *Behavior Therapy* 1 (1970): 33–50.
13. J. R. Cautela, "Covert Sensitization," *Psychological Reports* 20 (1967): 459–468.

14. J. R. Cautela, "Covert Conditioning, Assumptions and Procedures," *Journal of Mental Imagery* 1 (1977): 53–64.
15. J. R. Cautela, "Covert Sensitization."
16. A. E. Kazdin, "Effects of Covert Modeling and Model Reinforcement on Assertive Behavior," *Journal of Abnormal Psychology* 83 (1974): 240–252.
17. Moshe Feldenkrais, *Awareness Through Movement* (New York: Harper and Row, 1972), p. 129.
18. Richard M. Suinn, "Behavioral Rehearsal Training for Ski Racers," *Behavior Therapy* 3 (1972), no. 519.
19. Jerome L. Singer, "Fantasy: The Foundation of Serenity," *Psychology Today,* July 1976, p. 34.
20. Joseph E. Shorr, *Psycho-imagination Therapy* (New York: Intercontinental Medical Book Corp., 1972).

Chapter 11

1. Thomas F. Saarinen, "Student Views of the World," chapter in Robert M. Downs and David Stea, eds., *Image and Environment* (Chicago: Aldine, 1973).
2. J. Ross Mackay, "The Interactance Hypothesis and Boundaries in Canada: A Preliminary Study," *The Canadian Geographer* 3 (1958): 1–8.
3. T. R. Lee, "Brennan's Law of Shopping Behavior," *Psychological Reports* 11 (1962): 662.
4. Roger B. Potter, "Directional Bias Within the Usage and Perceptual Fields of Urban Consumers," *Psychological Reports,* 38 (1976): 988–990.
5. Ronald Briggs, "Urban Cognitive Distance," in Roger M. Downs and David Stea, eds., *Image and Environment* (Chicago: Aldine, 1973), pp. 361–388.
6. Albert Stevens, "The Role of Inference and Internal Structure in the Representation of Spatial Information" (Paper presented at Cartography Workshop, San Francisco, October 30, 1976).
7. Ulric Neisser, *Cognition and Reality* (San Francisco: W. H. Freeman, 1976), p. 108.
8. Ibid.

9. Jean Piaget and Barbel Inhelder, *L'image Mental Chez l'Enfant* (Paris: Presses Universitaires de France, 1966).

10. K. Lynch, *Image of the City* (Cambridge, Mass.: MIT Press, 1960).

11. K. Hooper, "Superfeatures of the U.C. Santa Cruz Environment" (Paper presented at the Cartography Workshop, San Francisco, October 29–31, 1976).

12. Stanley Milgram, et al., "A Psychological Map of New York City," *American Scientist* 60 (1972): 194–200.

13. Lynch, *Image of the City.*

14. David Ley, *The Black Inner City as a Frontier Outpost* (Ph.D. thesis, Pennsylvania State University, 1972).

15. Peter R. Gould, "On Mental Maps," *Michigan Inter-University Community on Mathematical Geographers,* Discussion Paper Number 9, 1966.

16. Patricia L. Brantingham and Paul J. Brantingham, "Residential Burglary and Urban Form," *Urban Studies* 12 (1975): 273–284.

17. F. N. Shemyakin, "Orientation in Space," in *Psychological Science in the USSR,* Vol. 1 (Washington: Office of Technical Services, 62-11083, 1962).

18. Michael Southworth, "The Sonic Environment of Cities," *Environment and Behavior* 1 (1969): pp. 49–70.

19. David Stea and Denis Wood, *A Cognitive Atlas: The Psychological Geography of Four Mexican Cities,* in press.

20. Roger M. Downs and David Stea, eds., *Image and Environment* (Chicago: Aldine Publishing Co., 1973), p. 11.

21. Yi-Fu Tuan, "Images of Mental Maps," *Annals of the Association of American Geographers* 65 (1975): 205–213.

22. Zenon W. Pylyshyn, "What the Mind's Eye Tells the Mind's Brain: A Critique of Mental Imagery," *Psychological Bulletin* 80 (1973): 1–24.

Chapter 12

1. E. B. Titchener, *Lectures on the Experimental Psychology of the Thought Processes* (New York: Macmillan, 1909), p. 8.

2. Lorna Simpson and P. McKellar, "Types of Synaesthesia," *Journal of Mental Science* 100 (1955): 422.
3. L. E. Marks, "Synthesia: The Lucky People with Mixed-Up Senses," *Psychology Today* 9 (1971): 50–55.
4. Peter McKellar, *Imagination and Thinking* (New York: Basic Books, 1957), p. 57.
5. Laszlo Moholy-Nagy, *Painting Photography Film* (Cambridge, Mass.: MIT Press, 1967), p. 15.
6. Yi-Fu Tuan, *Topophilia* (New York: Prentice-Hall, 1974).
7. W. H. Nault, "Children's Map Reading Abilities—A Need for Improvement," *Newsletter of the Geographic Society of Chicago* 3 (January 1967): 5.
8. Faber Birren, *Color Psychology and Color Therapy,* rev. ed. (New Hyde Park, N.Y.: University Books, 1961).
9. Henry Dreyfuss, *The Symbol Sourcebook* (New York: McGraw-Hill, 1972).
10. R. Sommer and M. Estabrook, "The Colored Compass," *International Journal of Symbology* 5 (1974): 37–51.
11. G. H. Kent and A. J. Rosanoff, "A Study of Association in Insanity," *American Journal of Insanity* 67 (1910): 37–96, 317–390. See also D. S. Palermo and J. J. Jenkins, *Word Association Norms: Grade School Through College* (Minneapolis: University of Minnesota Press, 1964).

Chapter 13

1. Donald Appleyard and Kenneth Craik, "The Berkeley Environmental Simulation Project," in T. G. Dickert and K. R. Domeny, eds., *Environmental Impact Assessment: Guidelines and Commentary* (Berkeley: University Extension, University of California, 1974), pp. 121–126.
2. Alton DeLong, "The Use of Scale Models in Spatial Behavioral Research," *Man-Environment Systems,* 1976–77, pp. 179–182.
3. Jerome Sirlin, *Composite Image Design System* (Department of Environmental Design, Cornell University, undated).

4. K. Hooper, "Superfeatures of the U.C. Santa Cruz Environment" (Paper presented at the Cartography Workshop, San Francisco, Oct. 29–31, 1976).

5. Rosemary Gordon, "A Very Private World," in P. W. Sheehan, *The Function and Nature of Imagery* (New York: Academic Press, 1972), pp. 63–80.

6. Ayn Rand, *The Fountainhead* (Philadelphia: Blakiston, 1943).

7. Steen E. Rasmussen, *Experiencing Architecture* (London: Chapman and Hall, 1959).

8. P. Thiel, "Notes on the Description, Scaling, Notation, and Scoring of Some Perceptual and Cognitive Attributes of the Physical Environment," in *Environmental Psychology,* H. Proshansky et al., eds. (New York: Holt, Rinehart, and Winston, 1970).